The
Beekay Guide
to Carp Baits

Ken Townley

First published in 1998
Beekay International Publishers
Withy Pool, Bedford Road,
Henlow, Beds SG16 6EA
Tel: 01462 816960

Printed in Great Britain at The Bath Press, Bath.

Contents

1. An Introduction to Carp Baits

There is no doubt that many newcomers to carp angling today find the subject of carp baits confusing and, at times, downright frustrating. This is often because the subject is surrounded with a mystique all of its own, with a unique jargon and a sub-culture of secrecy and misinformation aimed at creating that very confusion and frustration. In this book I hope to be able to get to the heart of carp baits for both the newcomer and the experienced angler as I explain the various aspects of carp bait and cut through the cloak of jargon and 'heavy chemistry' that seems to surround the subject at times. Hopefully by the time you have finished reading this book you will be able to put together a bait or devise a baiting strategy that will stand you in good stead no matter where you are fishing, be it on a small easy stockie lake, or on a lightly stocked, massive inland sea such as Wraysbury.

The list of items that can and will catch carp is seemingly endless. Seeds, particles, natural baits, boilies, they are all successful to varying degrees, depending on the water you are fishing and the pressure to which it has been subjected, but though carp anglers have been pretty adventurous at times in the past, we can be still be accused of being rather limited in our thinking and approach at times. Having stated that there are loads of carp baits, I have to say that I am a boilie man: I make no bones about my preference for boiled baits first and foremost. I prefer fishing with boilies simply because, over the years that I have been fishing, boiled baits have put more carp on the bank for me than any other type of bait. That is not to say that I don't use an alternative bait if I feel it is likely to be more successful, but I am convinced that boilies catch more and bigger fish in the long run.

A boiled bait mounted on a hair rig is about as efficient a way of catching carp as you can get, but do not risk becoming blinkered in your approach. It pays to keep an open mind about your tactics and bait. For instance, these days most carp anglers regard sweetcorn as old hat, but witness the success of flavoured sweetcorn on hard fished waters all around the country. Pre-flavoured and dyed tinned sweetcorn has been very successful on many waters where most carp men would tell you that any form of sweetcorn was a hopeless failure.

I find that many anglers fall into the trap of thinking that they have to follow the latest trend, often to the detriment of their own results. They are looking for a quick fix but they are often likely to be disappointed. Of course, if you look at the results of others fishing your favourite lake and they all seem to be catching well on one particular bait, then you'd be silly to use anything else, but you should bear in mind that the more fish get caught on that bait, the sooner it is that they will begin to wise up and avoid it. By joining the rest of the crowd you could actually

1

The author Ken Townley, looking happy with a mid-30 (16.4Kg).

help to hasten the end of a bait's run of success. It is at times like these when the experienced carp man needs to use his loaf. If he is the first to switch to an alternative bait he may get the one jump on the other guys on the lake.

In this book I hope to outline for you not only the history, development and latest advances in all types of base mixes and ingredients, but also take a look at important alternative baits that may be effective, for as we all know, carp baits don't just revolve around one approach. The offshoots of the carp bait scene are many and varied and include flavours and sweeteners, colours and enhancers, liquid foods and powdered extracts, amino acids and enzymes. The subject can be as complex or as simple as you wish to make it: it's up to you how far down the road you wish to travel, but I think that only by acquiring as wide an understanding of the subject as possible will a carp angler be able to excel in his sport.

Many newcomers to carp fishing find the whole business of boilie making too full of technical jargon and long winded mumbo-jumbo. It's true that if you want to get involved in the study of attraction and the more complex formulation of protein baits you need to have a simple understanding of science, but more important is an understanding of fish behaviour. Many of the most successful carp anglers in the country freely admit that they neither know nor care about the more technical aspects of carp baits, but their knowledge of how carp feed and what influences them to do so is second to none. As far as their bait is concerned, they stick to what they know best by offering a well formulated, pleasant smelling boiled bait that they know the carp will eat in quantity. Their bait may be based on fishmeals, birdfoods, milk proteins, enzyme treated hydrolysates or any old rubbish they can get their hands on. The prime ingredient that goes into their bait is CONFIDENCE! Their experience over the years has taught them what catches and what does not: when they make up a bait they are 100% confident that it will catch and there is no better starting point in carp fishing.

A common mistake made by anglers just getting started in carp fishing is to compare the way we taste with the way carp do so. While, to a certain extent, if a boilie tastes good to us it will also taste good to a carp, that doesn't always hold true. Carp are known to respond to feeding stimuli that would taste appallingly bitter to our palates, and can you imagine yourself eating earthworms, maggots, raw freshwater mussels or mouthfuls of silt-covered bloodworm? A carp has a remarkably Catholic range of acceptable tastes and smells, far more wide ranging than humans, and we should accept that bitter and unpleasant foodstuffs (to we humans) make up a large part of a carp's diet. However, they are also very happy eating sweet-tasting food items such as some boilies and particles; confusing, isn't it?

A similar illogical comparison is often expressed regarding the carp's sense of smell. In humans we are limited to a very narrow range of smells that come to us through our nasal passages. In carp the sense of smell is many times more receptive than ours, and their smell organs – the olfactory membranes – are thousands of times more sensitive than ours. In addition, a carp's sense of smell is finely tuned towards receiving messages from chemical stimuli that its instincts recognise as food. These instincts are with them from the first day of life. They have no outside influences to tell them what they can or cannot eat; no mum or dad to say, "Eat your greens, they are good for you!"

Carp have to fend for themselves from Day One and their highly developed feeding instincts are the result of millions of years of evolution. We, on the other hand are well known for eating things that are not good for us. Most of us only care if a food item tastes good and smells good, not if it does us any good.

Ask yourself this, would you pour crushed garlic, loads of fish oil and some salt over a plate of peaches and cream? Of course you wouldn't, so, naturally enough, if you are comparing a human sense of smell with that of a carp, you would never dream of putting, say, a strong strawberry flavour in a fishmeal base mix. But why not? Though many anglers have trouble reconciling the thought of a sweet, fruity smell with the savoury and slightly bitter smell and taste of most fish-meals, it doesn't follow that carp react in the same way. Just because it seems an awful prospect to you, don't think that strawberry flavoured fish meals don't catch carp. They do! And what about that garlic concoction on your plate of peaches? One of the most effective flavour signals of all time has been the Peach Melba/garlic essential oil/fish feed oil combination used on the Premier Baits original fishmeal base mix. It is yet another example showing just how easy it is to make the mistake of comparing a carp's sense of smell and taste with our own. Sure, you would probably never even think of putting fresh strawberries and cream on your morning kipper but a carp might!

As part of the understanding of what makes a good carp bait, we have to look in some detail at the way carp feed and how they receive their food messages underwater. By making your bait as attractive to a carp as you can, you hope that your quarry will be fooled into thinking that your bait is food and pick it up. You also have to introduce a sufficient quantity to keep its interest going once the first sample has been tried. This brings me to the nub of the whole subject of carp baits – attraction and nutrition.

Imagine this: you soak a small cork ball in neat flavour for 24 hours, then put it onto a pop-up rig and cast it in front of a visible, patrolling carp. The carp, sensing the presence of a stimulating food message investigates, finds the source and sucks it in. Result? One well-hooked carp in the landing net. The carp was turned on, then fooled, by the food message from the cork ball. But suppose you flavoured thousands of cork balls with the same food message and introduced them to the lake; how many do you think the carp would eat before it realised that all it was devouring was cork? Not many, I can tell you! I hope that example will outline the basic difference between attractor baits (attraction) and food baits (nutrition). Don't worry if you are not sure about the terminology right now, by the time you finish this book, that uncertainty will have disappeared.

Carp fishing is big business these day, and carp baits take up a large proportion of that business. This book is not intended for those guys who have been there, done that. They've been fishing for thirty years and have seen them come and seen them go. These guys probably know more than I could teach them in any case. Nor is the book aimed at the carp addict who has got all the books and all the mags, (did you know that there are now seven magazine titles with the word 'carp' in them on sale in the UK today?), who has read every article ever written about bait and knows it all...or at least, thinks he does! Come to think of it, if that's what he has done, he'll probably be more confused than a relative newcomer to the sport!

The advice offered herein is aimed more at the guy who wants to know that little bit more; who wants to get more involved, who wants to acquire a greater fund of knowledge and a more buoyant confidence in his own ability to catch carp. For a cover price just a bit more than the cost of three issues of the technical carp fishing titles, I hope this book will be the key to that extra knowledge and confidence. In these pages I shall deal with all the various ingredients that make up the most popular types of carp bait. I shall take an in-depth look at attractors, various foodstsuffs, particles and groundbaits. I shall also be looking at more advanced types of bait and at the most recent developments on the bait scene.

Just a quick note on the measurements used in the book. I have used metric measurements throughout. The kids reading the book will find nothing at all strange about this as they've been taught to accept metrics for years, but for all those the old foggies out there, please try to think of 25g as roughly equalling an ounce and 500g as being a rough equivalent to a pound.

OK. Let's start our journey toward what I hope will be a better understanding of the world of carp baits. If you have any problems in your own mind by the time you finish this book I will have failed in my job...and I don't intend to do that!

2. A Beginners Guide to Carp Baits

In the U.K. no other subject generates such intense debate among carp anglers as bait. Many actually consider the ability to make top quality, highly nutritious boiled baits to be the single most important factor contributing towards their success. Others favour relatively simple, low nutrition baits, which also have the advantage of being comparatively cheap. Advocates of this point of view claim that that there is no need to use complex or expensive baits to catch carp. They may have a point, but experience has shown that carp which are subject to heavy angling pressure soon stop eating inferior baits.

The general concensus of opinion is that nutritional baits which provide a supplement to the carp's natural food and thus some form of nutritional benefit are far more effective, both in the short and long term. It is no coincidence that most of the big fish landed from our lakes and rivers each season fall to good quality baits. I fish in France quite a bit and each time I visit, the more carp specialists I see on the bankside. Carp fishing in France has undergone something of a revolution over the last decade. The modern specialist techniques introduced by English anglers visiting the big-fish waters such as the Lac de St Cassien have quickly been adopted by French carp men, making carp more catchable and more accessible to the average French angler. To start with I used relatively simple, cheap and cheerful baits but as the pressure on French carp has increased, it has become clear that better baits catch better carp.

I'm sure you don't need me to tell you that modern carp fishing relies to a great extent on two important factors, namely, bait and the hair rig. The hair rig was developed in 1980 by Lenny Middleton and Kevin Maddocks as a way of overcoming the carp's suspicion of nylon line and heavy weights. As I'm sure you know, the hair allows the bait to be attached to the hook by a length of very light nylon line, leaving the hook bare, thus making hook penetration so much easier.

The hair was designed to be fished in conjunction with hard, boiled baits, usually made up to the angler's own secret recipe, containing various attractors and stimulants to encourage carp to feed on the bait. The more sophisticated baits were stunningly successful and quickly became the first choice. Anglers who ignored the latest developments were soon left behind by those who took the time and effort to exploit the quickly changing bait world.

The formulation of complex carp baits has been elevated almost to a science. Whether or not this is necessary is debatable and it is unlikely that any two carp anglers will agree totally on one particular approach, but the conflicting arguments need to be considered equally, for only then can the angler form an opinion as to the merits of one particular bait over another.

Let's consider the two sides of the argument. On the one hand, there are those who favour baits of High Nutritional Value (HNV), claiming that success lies in creating a balanced nutritional bait containing all the carp's food requirements in one go. These are protein, fats, carbohydrates, vitamins and minerals. Such a bait is then introduced in sufficient quantity to ensure that the fish come to regard it as a natural food source which will supplement their natural diet...you hope!

On the other hand there are those who say that all a boiled bait needs to do is attract and entice a carp to eat it, without competing with or even supplementing natural food items. Both approaches have their merits, but whichever approach you decide upon, you must be 100% sure that your bait is acceptable and palatable enough to be picked up and eaten by carp, possibly in great quantities.

The list of ingredients that have been used to make boiled baits is seemingly endless but many anglers these days prefer to buy a mix that simply requires the addition of eggs and a flavour followed by boiling to produce finished baits. There are several English bait firms now supplying mixes to the shops and by mail order and all offer sophisticated, tried and tested recipes that will catch carp.

Mind you, the angler who prefers to formulate his own mixes using recipes of his own design and choice is probably going to get the most enjoyment out of making and using his baits. He may use high nutritional value baits based on expensive, but highly nutritious milk or egg proteins, or he might prefer making protein baits using fish, animal or vegetable proteins. These are often more coarse, less refined products, but they are still nutritious enough to formulate HNV baits.

Alternatively there are baits that rely on their high level of fat, both as an attractor and to provide a nutritional message. These are often referred to as high energy baits, so called because it is known that carp derive most of their expendable energy from poly-unsaturated fats. High energy baits are often based upon feeds like calf milk powders, birdfoods such as canary seed mixes and other bird feeds designed to keep racing pigeons in top class condition.

Finally there are the low value baits based on soya flour and semolina. These have little or no food value and catch fish solely on the strength of liquid flavours and enhancers that are added to attract and stimulate carp into feeding, but they are ideal as ingredients for attractor baits.

I feel it is important to understand how carp feed and the way they are attracted to their food sources. In human terms I suppose we'd talk of smell and taste, yet as I have mentioned previously, it is a huge mistake to attribute human terms to carp, as their way of detecting their food is much more complex than ours. Their feeding triggers come from natural food items, and carp rely on these to find their food, so it makes sense to try and mimic natural stimuli within our bait in order to attract the carp to it and hopefully to feed upon it, which is why we include attractors and feeding stimulants such as commercial flavours in the baits.

I do feel that there is such a thing as a logical progression in carp baits. By that I mean that there is no point in tackling virgin fish with the most sophisticated bait at your disposal when you could catch them on a very simple bait such as sweetcorn. On the other hand, I feel sure that carp that are subject to extensive angling pressure quickly become wary of inferior quality baits. This is when the more aware, bait-conscious, carp anglers will switch to nutritionally superior baits in the hope that the carp can be persuaded to regard their offerings as a source of natural food rather than yet another purely artificial bait.

Less than a decade ago most beginners would have started carp fishing using a bait of their own making, probably using a friend's jealously guarded, secret recipe. Today the newcomer to carp fishing is most likely to tackle the sport for the first time using a preserved boiled bait bought straight off the shelf of his local tackle shop. These baits, known as ready-mades, are convenient, effective and time-saving. There is a chapter dedicated to ready-made baits later on in the book.

There are a great many bait firms making ready-mades these days and among the market leaders in the ready-made bait market are the ranges from Nutrabaits and K.M. Professional Boilies. These well preserved, strong flavoured baits have accounted for an enormous number of massive fish for thousands of anglers in the UK and abroad. Witness the staggering success of Kevin Maddocks' superb catches from a wide variety of French and English waters. All of Kevin's success can be attributed to his own KM Professional ready-made range of baits; he rarely uses anything else.

I too use preserved ready-made baits on my French trips often in combination with an equal amount of home made baits. I recall fishing a short session on a lake in northern France during which we caught over 50 carp, all over 15lb (6,8kg) in weight up to a maximum of 32lb (14.5kg). They all fell to a combination of strawberry-flavoured Enervite boilies, in conjunction with KM Professional Strawberry ready-mades.

Knowing what I do about the carp bait business, it always amazes me just how effective ready-mades can be, bearing in mind that many of these types of bait are not really a nutritional bait in any sense of the word, but, boy, do they catch carp! I believe that many ready-mades catch primarily due to the strength of their flavours. Nutritionally the baits are fairly basic but the attractors within them are superb, among the very best. Being of limited food value, the carp need to eat a lot of bait in order to gain any nutritional satisfaction. This means that they will need to stay feeding on the bait carpet for a long time.

Mind you, carp do know what is good for them, and will eventually stop wasting energy looking for baits with little or no nutritional value...which is where the nutritional, food bait, base mixes come into their own.

Recently, ready-mades have taken something of a leap forward with the release of the new K.M. and Nutrabaits ranges of ready-mades. Both these companies have been trying to improve the nutritional quality of their baits by increasing the amount of nutritious ingredients used in them and their latest offerings are much more valid as food baits than many alternatives.

Preserved ready-made baits have a lot going for them in terms of nutrition, attraction and, most importantly, in convienience. The amount of time you can save by using ready-made baits can much more profitably be spent carp fishing! However, they are not cheap; to create a baiting programe using them alone would cost a fortune. This is why I suggest using a good ready-made in combination with your own, home made baits, but all in all I'd suggest that the preserved boilies you can buy ready for use off the tackle dealer's shelf, are among some of the best carp baits available.

3. Flavours and other Attractors

We refer to attractors when we speak of a product we add to a bait in order to entice carp to think it may be food and then to pick it up. Attractors come in many forms, but in this chapter I want to take a general look at some of the most popular.

FLAVOURS

Attraction is THE watchword in any carp bait and the easiest way to make any bait attractive is to give it an artificial flavour that somehow mimics a naturally occurring underwater source of attraction that the carp have come to recognise as food. There is nothing new in flavours; they have been used in carp baits since the mid-60s but as far as attraction goes there are some recent developments that have taken carp attraction forward a long way.

You might think that there is nothing new left to be discovered in the big wide world of flavours, but you'd be wrong. Some of the most significant advances on the bait scene have been in the field of flavours.

The food industry is continually striving to improve their already extensive range of artificial flavours and the results of their labours eventually find their way into the catalogues of the top bait companies. Some of the newest additions to those catalogues are often flavour blends that have been shown to be more attractive to carp than a single flavour on its own.

Of course, it has to be remembered that carp are not actually responding to the smell of the flavour, but rather to its chemical signal, which, we assume, mimics in some way, a naturally occurring stimulus that they find in the course of their everyday search for food. In addition the acidic nature of most flavours generates a slight change in the chemical properties of the lake water surrounding the bait and it is this localised pH change that carp find so attractive. Most localised fluctuations in pH will be investigated by carp to discover if the change indicates a food source.

The business end of a carp is very highly tuned towards detecting chemical signals from food. The olfactory membranes are the most important senses carp possess.

It is widely argued that carp, unlike humans, can use their senses to assess the taste as well as the smell of food before they even take it into their mouth. Though their primary taste organs are situated in their cheeks and possibly, to a certain

9

extent, in their barbules, it is thought that they can also assess a food for its smell and taste by passing water infused with the chemical signals from the food over their olfactory membranes.

Before I go any further I'd just like to take a closer look at the chemical make up and the attractive properties of flavours to try and explain what makes a good flavour.

It has long been known that excessive flavour levels can work against the carp angler by actually becoming repulsive rather than attractive once the acceptable dosage has been exceeded. As a rule a maximum of 5ml/500g has proved to be a good guide, though many flavours, particularly the cheese flavours, actually work at their best at levels as low as 1ml/500g, and some essential oils are used at one drop/500g!

However, there seem to be exceptions to this rule and some flavours can be used at levels of twice or even three times the 5ml level. Most vanilla, cream and butter flavours contain substances known as esters – individual chemicals that in combination make up an artificial smell – that can be tolerated at comparatively high levels and some of the best results using maple flavour were made at levels of 15-20ml/500g. Yet if you were to use such a high level of, say, cheese flavour or bun spice flavour you would soon find that the carp would not tolerate such a dose for long and that a lower level was more effective.

Remember that the flavour that smells so appealing to you is only a purely chemical signal to the carp. How many times have you seen anglers at carp angling exhibitions open bottle after bottle of flavour, eventually buying the ones that have the most attractive smell in human terms. That's not very logical, is it? Surely it would be far more logical if anglers were to select a flavour on the basis of its chemical appeal to the carp rather than to their own much less sensitive noses.

These chemically attractive smells are called esters and simple esters include amyl acetate (pear drop smell) and ethyl butrate (pineappple smell), both of which are commonly used in fruit flavours. The chemical reaction whereby esters are formed is called esterfication and the reaction involves an acid and an alcohol. It is because of this reaction that most synthetic flavours have a low pH value. This acidic pH is what gives some flavours a bitter, burning sensation to the tongue.

Sweeteners are one of the most common substances used to counteract this burning taste and as most sweeteners are actually on the alkaline side of the pH scale they tend to be very effective at adjusting the pH of the bait towards a more acceptable point for the carp.

Esters are mixed with a solvent in varying quantities to form the finished bottle of flavour that you receive from your favourite bait supplier. The most common solvents are: propylene glycol, isopropyl alcohol, ethyl alcohol, glycerol, diacetin, triacetin and refined or unrefined oils.

The least commonly used solvents in everyday use are glycerol and ethyl alcohol. To a certain extent this is because they are expensive, but in the case of glycerol its thickness and lack of viscosity (its ability to mix and flow) are unpopular with the food industry for most applications. However, glycerol based flavours are excellent carp attractors, the reason being that their underlying sweetness takes all the agression out of otherwise acidic flavours, without excessively changing its acidic signal, which is what the carp find so attractive in the first place. It is this rather bland, though slightly sweet taste, which makes them more palatable than the sharper tasting flavours based on solvents such as propylene glycol.

More and more bait companies are now adding glycerol based flavours to their ranges but one company whose flavours are almost exclusively based on glycerol is the UK market leader Nutrabaits. The range of fruit, spice and specialist flavours on offer from this company are some of the most acceptable on the market.

Lots of the UK's top carp anglers are now using glycerol based flavours, not just because they are more acceptable to carp but also due to what we call 'solvent blow-out'.

Many flavours are based upon cheap, commonly used solvents such as propylene glycol and isopropyl alcohol. Regardless of the actual chemical formula of the flavour, a significant chemical signal will always come from the solvent. At first this is not a problem, but after a while the carp begin to become suspicious of the smell of the solvent itself and no matter what combination of esters is used, if the resulting flavour is based upon the same solvent, there is a real danger that the carp will become wary of that solvent regardless of the effectiveness of the flavour esters.

So in addition to paying careful attention to your choice of flavour, remembering that some ester combinations work much better than others, you should also look carefully at the solvent upon which the flavour is based. Most of the reputable bait companies give details of the solvent base on the label of the bottle. Glycerol based flavours may be more expensive than propylene glycol based ones but generally they are more effective because they have a much more acceptable taste.

Unfortunately glycerol is a thick, low viscosity liquid and is less soluble in colder water than other solvents. This brings me to the next best solvent currently available, ethyl alcohol. To many, ethyl alcohol is the perfect all-year solvent. It has no noticeable smell and its chemical signal is very acceptable to carp. The big

A glycerol-based flavour and an essential oil

advantage of this particular solvent is that it is highly volatile, with excellent solubility, thus mixing freely with water regardless of the water's temperature. The result is a faster, more effective flavour leak, epecially in winter when glycerol based flavours may be less effective due to the comparative insolubility of the solvent.

A significant characteristic of ethyl alcohol based flavours is their fresh, clean smell, though their taste tends to be rather sharp. This sharpness can easily be overcome by using sweeteners.

Many bait companies now offer flavours based on ethyl alcohol, though Nutrabaits is unique in offering the same ester blends on both glycerol and ethyl alcohol. This means that you can stick to the same flavour throughout the year without having to worry that your glycerol based flavour (more effective in summer) will lose its potency in the winter (when ethyl alcohol may be more effective).

Some of the most recent developments are flavours based on natural extracts. These are expensive and are not in common use, but they are set to take the carp world by storm. One that has been astonishingly successful has been Caviar flavour from Nutrabaits, a flavour actually extracted from the natural product. It is horrendously expensive but to the best of my knowledge it has accounted for at least three fifty pound (22.7kg) carp from British waters. In all cases the natural flavour was blended with another type of attractor, which brings me to another recent delevlopment in the formulation of carp baits in the UK.

ESSENTIAL OILS

An increasing trend towards mixing flavours with essential oils has marked the mid-1990s. When essential oils first became generally available they were almost entirely used in isolation. However, many anglers now like to blend individual mixtures of flavour and essential oil to form their own unique attractors. There are a great many combinations that work well and all of them seem to be more effective than either the oil or the flavour if used on its own. You may also like to consider making up your own blends of two or three flavours, two or three essential oils, or any combination you care to dream up. Such blends would produce an attractor unique to yourself, but while this MAY work, there is no guarantee that every combination you invent is likely to succeed.

But there is no getting away from the fact that flavour/essential oil blends are all the rage at the moment, and with good reason. The permutations are practically endless and are limited only by your own pioneering spirit. As a general rule I would suggest that you use as a starting point half the recommended inclusion levels printed on both bottles. In other words, if the recommended dose of the flavour is 6ml/500g and that of the essential oil is 12 drops/500g, I would suggest that you start off at 3ml of the flavour and 6 drops of the essential oil. You will be able to judge the effectiveness – or lack of it - of these levels after a few trips and you can then adjust them as you think suitable.

A new step forward on the UK's ready-made bait market has been two new baits from Nutrabaits. As they were the first to pioneer the use of flavour and essential oils blends in their base mixes, it comes as no surprise that a couple of the new range of ready made boilies also contain some of the most effective blends yet discovered. The blending of flavours and essential oils came as a natural extension to the blending of either two flavours or two essential oils. One of the most

Ken Townley with a fabulous linear mirror of 30.5 pounds (13.9kg).

A 40 pound (18.2kg) common to Carole Townley.

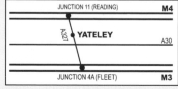

successful flavour combinations of all time is Strawberry and Cream. Don't ask me why this should be, but there is something very special about the chemical signal that this blend gives off underwater. If you have never tried this super-blend I strongly advise you to give it a go.

By coincidence, glycerol acts as an emulsifier on oils which means that blends of glycerol-based flavours and essential oils are self-emulsifying.

While blends of flavours and oils are the 'in' thing at present, blends of essential oils alone can be equally successful. You can really let your hair down and indulge yourself as much as you like, but always bear in mind that occasionally a blend may not work as well as individual flavours or oils. It is a rare occurence but it does happen sometimes.

My favourite blend of essential oils is a 2:1 mixture of Geranium and Clove oils. I find it easier to make up a 2ml bottle of the blend and then use 8 drops of the mixture. This seems to be the most effective level.

Other successful blends include Thyme and Geranium oils, Ginger and Sage oils, Euclayptus and Peppermint oils and Spearmint and Black Pepper oils. I have no idea why these blends should work so well, all I can assume is that in some way their chemical properties form a smell that in some way mimics a natural or stimulating signal that carp find attractive.

LIVER-BASED ATTRACTORS

Some of the most important steps forward lately have been in the field of powdered and liquid natural extracts. One of the first purely natural products to be used by the carp world was liver. Powdered liver, liquid liver, liver extract and concentrated liver have all been used to enhance and improve the nutritional qualities of carp baits and with good reason. Liver is absolutely stuffed full of most of the essential amino acids necessary for life. Carp love its taste and its smell. Liver does them good and they seem to know it. It can be used at just about any level in any type of mix. You can even add pure liver that has been liquidised in a food processor to your mix, knowing that it will improve any mix considerably.

After the initial experiments in the early 70s, liver did not take long to catch on and I know that some of the best catches have been made using a liver extract of some kind. There are now liver flavours available that smell just like the real thing.

LIQUID FOODS

The nutritional properties of liquid liver as a food for elderly and infirm hospital patients is well documented. Some liquid food additives currently used in carp baits were originally formulated for use in old peoples' homes and hospitals to help patients who have difficulty assimilating protein into their diet. Such products include Minamino and Phosphorylcolamine. These are liver-based but they also contain a host of other natural extracts to supplement the overall nutritional balance of the liquid food.

The bait firms now sell a wide range of liquid foods, mostly based on the medicinal products mentioned above. For instance, Multimino-PPC from Nutrabaits is one of the best liquid foods currently on offer to anglers. Others include the Sense Appeal range, Nutramino and Carpmino.

Another excellent food liquid is Corn Steep Liquor which is derived from the grain of the maize plant. It has a well defined and consistent amino acid profile and a high level of complex sugars that produce a very attractive smell and taste. Because of its origin it is best used as a soak for maize but it can also be added to any base mix at the rate of 10-15ml/500g. Nutrabaits and Mainline feature Corn Steep Liquor in their range.

All the natural food liquids can be very effective as a soak. My favourite is Multimino-PPC. This product has been blended in such a way as to form a cloud just off the bottom of the lake. I have been using Multimino-PPC soaks for a couple of years now and one of my most successful recipes is chopped boilies combined with small pellets, soaked in 30-50ml of Multimino. The mixture is used primarily as a groundbait because the pellets break down quite quickly forming a mass of tiny particles on the bottom with the red cloud of liquid attractor floating just off the bottom.

VITAMIN AND MINERAL SUPPLEMENTS

Liquid kelp, powdered kelp and dried granules of seaweed may seem peculiar additions to carp baits but in the UK these products are very highly rated. Dried seaweed is a product that I first discovered about six years ago. It is designed as a vitamin and mineral supplement for racing and show horses. It can be used at low levels in any type of mix, though I have found it blends particularly well with fishmeal and birdfood baits. About 15-20g added to 500g of base mix is enough to add a sparkle to your bait by improving its vitamin and mineral content.

Carp are very aware of the need to maintain the right balance of these two vital nutritional materials and their food senses are highly tuned towards locating any source of vitamins and minerals. In other words they can smell these dietary requirements in your bait and seaweed is therefore a perfect additive.

Powdered kelp is yet another product that performs a similar function. It was on the 'secret' list in the UK for many years before becoming more widely available in 1996. One of the first bait companies to use a powdered kelp in their mixes was the firm Premier Baits. Their fish meal base mixes containing powdered kelp are some of the most successful of all time.

Liquid kelp is just another variation on a theme. It is quite likely that carp can detect a liquid ingredient in a bait faster than they can a powdered or solid one, as they leak from a boilie much quicker than do solids. You can therefore get the best of both worlds by including both liquid and powdered kelp in a bait. The liquid will act as a primary (smell) attractor, the powder as a secondary (taste) attractor.

If you can find liquid kelp in your tackle shop give it a try in your usual mix. I think you will see a significant improvement. I suggest a level of 10-15ml/500g, though there is considerable room for experiment here.

MARINE EXTRACTS

You will probably have heard about mussel, shrimp and lobster extracts. I have used all three but in my opinion Green Lipped Mussel Extract is head and shoulders above any other type of marine extract due to its much higher Betaine content and I'll deal with Betaine in more detail in a moment.

Green Lipped Mussel extract has a superb smell and taste and is a perfect supplement to any mix. It has a unique underwater attraction as well, which begins to leak from the bait almost immediately. Once a carp gets a sniff of Green Lipped Mussel extract, it's as good as hooked!

Some natural oils are highly stimulatory to carp and fish oils are probably the best of all. However, fish oils need to be used with a bit of caution as excessive amounts can cause problems in carp. We look at fish oils in more detail in the chapter on fishmeals.

Carp baits are evolving all the time. As I write I am currently testing many new products that may find their way onto the shelves in future. However, all reputable bait companies test and re-test all their products before releasing them and it is quite possible that some that I'm working on may not be successful. Two products that have proved pretty good in testing are salmon extract and a pure krill extract. I am confident that these will soon become more widely available as they have been used to catch some very good fish in the UK during the past twelve months.

BETAINE HYDROCHLORIDE (HCl)

A recent addition to the bait shelves in the UK is a chemical called Betaine Hydrochloride. This is the significant active ingredient that is found in Green Lipped Mussel extract as well as in a host of other naturally occurring foodstuffs. I first encountered this product ten years ago and used it with staggering effect in the UK, taking eighteen 'twenties' in three trips from two different lakes. Betaine has no noticeable smell or taste as far as we are concerned, but carp go crazy for it.

One of the hardest and most pressured carp waters in my region is Salamander Lake, a tiny lake of less than two acres. The carp are very suspicious of all carp baits, having been the target of anglers for the past twenty years or more. There are only fifteen or sixteen carp in the lake and because of its small size, they seem to be able to comunicate danger signals with each other whenever a carp is hooked and landed. As a rule it is unusual to get more than one chance every 24 hours: to take five 'twenties' in a 24-hour trip, as I did when I started using Betaine, was fantastic, but that is how good Betaine can be when you get it just right.

Betaine has been used for many years by fish nutritionists to improve pellets and other diets used for rearing trout and salmon for the table and by adding the right combination of amino acids to Betaine, manufacturers have been able to develop a much more attractive pellet. It is used in the same way in carp baits. Betaine is a naturally occuring substance found in tiny quantities in a variety of living things. It is found in plants, yeasts, fungi, mussels, the flesh of fish and in other crustacea, molluscs and invertebrae.

Betaine HCl can be used in any type of mix, but again my preference is for a fish meal base mix. However, it is sure to work equally well on birdfoods and protein baits, as well as on 50/50 mixes. In fact, Nutrabaits have recently released a new birdfood/milk protein base mix called the Four Seasons Mix which contains an in-built source of Betaine.

Now pure Betaine is on sale you can include it in your own mix. It is one of those products that needs to be used carefully. Put too much in and you'll spoil the effect, but get the level just right and you'll have them crawling up the rods. To my mind Betaine HCI is one of the finest attractors of all time.

So that's a general look at some of the attractors that we use in carp baits. Now we'll look at one way of applying them successfully, as attractor baits.

4. Nutrition and Attraction

A well tried and tested formula was developed by Kent carp anglers in the late 60s. It reasoned that the best carp bait is one that contains all the carp's nutritional requirements in one go. The theory goes that in time the fish comes to think of such a complete nutritional bait as part and parcel of its natural food chain, assuming that enough is introduced over a period of time. These baits have come to be regarded as FOOD BAITS.

They were the brain child of a guy called Fred Wilton and his principles were further developed and enhanced by Sheffield angler Tim Paisley duing the late 70s and early 80s. Baits formulated along these lines have come to be known as NUTRITIONAL BAITS and the process whereby carp – in theory – come to accept such offerings as natural food is now known as NUTRITIONAL RECOGNITION.

The question as to whether or not such nutritional recognition is or is not a reality is very difficult for the layman to answer. "Scientific gobbledegook", says one section of the carp angling fraternity; "unquestionably proven, case closed", states another. Unfortunately the subject is too complex for simple or dogmatic answers as it raises many theoretical questions that cannot clearly be defined nor answered. For myself, I am firmly of the opinion that carp can and DO recognise the food value of a bait, sometimes almost immediately, often within a few days of initial introduction, and certainly within a few weeks, given a steady and regular supply of such a bait. However, I do not want to get involved in the theoretical quagmire of debate that currently bogs down some of the bait experts in this country. It seems to me that for every stated view you will find someone to state the opposite, and for every fact that you think is proven, someone will come along with the evidence to disprove it!

Tim Paisley's early work on nutrition and nutritional recognition is usually regarded as definitive by those who subscribe to the theory – of which I am most definitely one – but even if you cannot bring yourself to accept nutritional recognition I would urge you to keep an open mind about it, especially when it comes to attractor baits. Let's face it, ALL foodstuffs have certain elemental properties of nutrition about them; even pure flour and water is nutritional to a degree. By applying the nature of underwater attraction to your baits you are attempting to pull carp down onto your hookbait using the hoped-for irresistibility of the attractors in the bait. You are not intending to fool the carp into thinking that your bait is a long term food, but are simply going for an instant hit, to get under its guard. By giving the bait an exaggerated nutritional signal your plan will be temporarily to fool the carp into THINKING that your bait is food, even though its instincts may be telling it that there is something not quite right about the smell that it has detected. It matters not at this stage whether your bait is nutritional in any way, shape or form.

It all comes back to the business of mimicking a natural stimuli in order to fool the carp in the short term. Do you remember the flavoured cork ball analogy I used earlier in the book? The principle of using a pure attractor bait is more or less the same. In other words, you are trying to imitate natural signals that will encourage a carp to pick up your bait because it thinks that it is food. If its feeding instincts were not triggered off by the smell and taste of your bait, then the carp simply wouldn't pick it up. You are trying to send the carp a message via your bait, saying 'this is food': that is the thinking behind ATTRACTOR BAITS.

By their very nature, pure attractor baits are only a short term solution. It is not sufficient to instil a feeling of hunger in a carp by setting off its instinctive reactions towards underwater stimuli, without reinforcing the initial message with the reality it infers. Using the cork ball analogy again, they would simply stop feeding on anything that did not back up the food signal with nutritional satisfaction. It can be argued that, if you offer an excess of junk food to a carp, eventually it will have the sense to stop eating it, whereas we do not! So if the food value of your bait is poor, or if it falls below an acceptable standard, then the carp will eventually stop eating it, despite the positive signals you are sending to it via your attractors and flavours. In effect it will choose to ignore those very instincts that you have worked so hard to trigger. I hope that you can by now see clearly that to ignore the nutritional quality of your bait is a mistake.

First, let us look briefly at the way carp feed for it is important to understand nature's underwater larders, the instincts that carp use to find their food, and the signals that attract them.

We've already mentioned the all-important food message that we are trying to build into our bait in the form of flavours or other attractors. This food message is clearly detectable underwater by the carp through their olfactory membranes – you can call them the carp's nostrils if you like. The membranes are situated behind the small holes situated either side of the carp's head just in front of its eyes. Carp constantly sample the lake water for the food message by passing water over their smell organs through these small holes. In nature a carp's food is either buried in silt or mud, suspended as tiny solid particles in the lake water, or clinging to underwater features such as weed beds or sunken trees. Other individual food items, such as snails and various types of mussel, form natural food larders which the carp learn to visit, in much the same way as we learn to go to the refrigerator for the milk, to the pub for a beer or to McDonalds for a Big Mac. Experience has taught us where to go in order to sample certain tastes and carp too learn by experience to find natural larders.

All living things emit chemical messages and carp have evolved into the perfect food detectors we know them to be by recognising which of these messages spells FOOD!

A carp feeds by smell and taste, the initial seeking out of a food item being done by smell. Its senses recognise a food source, and provided that the message is backed up by a complementary taste, the carp will feed on that food until it has satisfied its hunger. Any suitable attractor can be added to a bait in order to fool the carp into thinking that a foreign substance is a food source, simply because it smells like one. Even if the bait has no food value whatsoever, as long as it smells like food to the carp, it will sample it for taste and nutrition. If you could coat a small pebble with pure strawberry flavour, mount it on a simple hair rig, and put it into the path of a feeding carp, it would quite probably pick up the pebble and try

You can see the openings to the olfactory membranes – the carp's nose – just above and in front of the eyes.

to eat it. The hair rig hooks the fish, you play it out and land it, and you've had the success you were after, but that doesn't mean that you would bait up heavily with stones, does it? No carp in its right mind is going to eat loads of stones, no matter how good they may smell, but it might very well pick up the single flavoured stone purely because it smelt like food. I'm sorry to labour this point but it is important.

Which bring me around once again to point out that attractor baits have one serious flaw to them, namely that if you pre-bait with a bait containing an excessive flavour level it may well "blow out" (stop being eaten by the carp) before you even cast a hook bait into the water.

OK, you may say, I'll only use a single hookbait, that way the carp will have nothing to use as a comparison and they will be unable fully to assess the nutritional qualities – or the lack thereof – of my bait. In that case your location skills will have to be pretty sharply honed. Sure, you will almost definitely be able to draw carp from a wide area into your area with regular baiting of a NUTRITIONAL bait, but you are unlikely to attract a carp down onto your fishing area with a single high-attract hook bait unless you are spot on their patrol route. In other words, you may be making life harder for yourself than it needs to be.

Carp anglers are suckers for smells in much the same way as the match boys are suckers for floats. Nothing so occupies their minds as flavours and other attractors. You only need to go to the Carp Society conference or attend the regional meetings to see what I mean. Crowds of eager aficionados can be seen standing around the bait displays, avidly sniffing at the hundreds of bottles of magic potions on offer. Indeed you will almost certainly have been one of the sniffers yourself! The fact that your own sense of smell will have been swamped by excessive flavour chemicals from the word go, does not prevent you opening and sniffing at a myriad of products and assessing their worth as a carp attractor...a pointless exercise, if ever there was one. A flavour or attractor may smell superb in the bottle but it may also be completely useless as an attractor. That is why the top bait companies always field test their products extensively before putting them onto the market. As a field tester for Nutrabaits I can tell you that I have used some absolute non-starters in the past that, thankfully, never found their way onto the market.

The list of potential attractors would need a book to itself and while all of them may or may not attract carp to your bait, not all are necessarily as successful as their manufacturers would wish.

Your individual choice of carp bait attractors is very important. Some attractors may have a strong enough signal to last long enough for you to achieve a short term result of two or three months. Others may last only for a light pre-baiting and the trip that follows. Then the bait blows and you need to look for another attractor. It is a vicious circle that keeps going around and around; short term gain followed by long term blow-out, followed by constant search for a viable alternative.

Yet it seems to me that a great many anglers I meet on the bank fish this way. Their cupboards are filled to bursting point with bottles of flavour, many of which have only had one or two doses taken out.

But, if you were aiming to produce a food message to complement a long term bait, you would not need to change the flavour for several years, assuming that the bait was of sufficient nutritional value that the carp would continue eating over such a long period.

So this presents another problem with attractor baits. You have to keep switching to something new, or something that was effective long enough ago for the carp to have forgotten that the particular smell spelt danger. This is where a combination of attractors may well be more suitable, as opposed to just a single flavour or attractor. A mixture of various smells may well mask the underlying one that caused the carp's downfall before and the carp fails to recognise the smell of danger.

You will note that I have tried to separate flavours from attractors. Sure, flavours ARE attractors, but not all attractors are flavours. Indeed, attractors do not even need to be in liquid form in order to give added power to the bait. That is not to say that flavours don't attract; some clearly do, but if you insist on thinking in terms only of flavours to add attraction to your bait, you are limiting your options severely. For many years this blinkered thinking was responsible for poor catches on many British waters, and it wasn't until respected anglers such as Tim Paisley, Bill Cottam and Julian Cundiff began to write so authoritatively about attractor baits that people began to open their eyes and see the possibilities of alternative attractors, and as the popularity of carp fishing grows so the problem of choice and alternatives becomes exaggerated.

When you go to a busy water that has seen heavy angling pressure, with thousands of boilies and buckets of grains and particles going in every summer, containing a mind-blowing number of differents attractors – mainly flavours – it is obviously difficult to know what has been used on the water before, and at what levels the flavours and other enhancers have been used. Maybe your favourite flavour has been used to excessive levels and has "blown" as a result. Under extreme pressure, maybe even the flavour solvent has become a source of suspicion.

As I mentioned earlier, liquids are not the only form of attractors. You can still keep the overall cost of your bait down by using 50% semolina as a base to your mix, but the simple addition of a range of other products such as dried yeast, liver powder, fishmeals, crushed hemp, maize meal, soya flour and ground canary food can turn a base mix with little or no solid attraction into one with much more pulling power. Even a small amount of milk or fish protein will add considerably to the effectiveness of a bait.

I would never make up a bait mix without including amino acids. Aminos are one of the key components of any attractor package. Carp can easily identify amino acids and they recognise and associate them with the presence of food and the quickest way to introduce the smell of amino acids into the water is through the use of liquid food additives. Carp simply adore the smell and the taste of these products, and not only that, they do them good as well. Most liquid foods also contain essential vitamins and minerals as well as other important feeding triggers such as sugars and enzyme extracts. These are by far the best sources of the food message that we are trying to send the carp and though they can be rather expensive, I strongly advise you to take the time and trouble to find a suitable product, whether it be though a bait dealer, your local fishing tackle shop, or from a chemist's shop.

You should bear in mind however, that even the best bait in the world is no good unless you put it in the places carp are likely to feed or on an observable patrol route. You have got to go to the fish when using attractor baits, rather than try to draw them to you. Get the attractors right and cast the bait to a well known area and a carp will in all probability have a good look at it. However, get the attractor strength wrong, usually by over-loading flavours and sweeteners, and you'll actually repel the carp from the bait rather than attract the fish to it.

You can usually tell if you have put too much flavour into your baits (or into your groundbait for that matter) when you get absolutely no action from your buzzers while carp are showing close to and over your baits with monotonous regularity.

There is nothing so frustrating as to watch carp, obviously excited by the smell of the bait carpet, not getting anywhere near your hook bait. Fish may be rolling and crashing out over the baits, but you are getting no action whatsoever at your end. The level of attraction is so strong that there is no turn-on where the baits are lying, but a lovely smell of food at the surface, right where you don't want it.

Attractor baits rely entirely on smell to catch carp. If the bait smells of food and the carp is close enough to get a whiff then it will probably investigate the source of the smell. As a method of catching carp it is limited and rather hit and miss. Far better to establish the food message and then back it up with a bait that is also a food in its own right. The more a carp eats a specific food – or bait – the easier it is to catch.

CARP BOOKS
THE BEEKAY GUIDES

Beekay Guide to 2000 British & European Carp Waters
Edited by Kevin Maddocks & Peter Mohan **£14.95**

Beekay Guide to Carp Rigs
Kevin Maddocks & Julian Cundiff **£9.99**

Beekay Guide To Starting Carp Fishing
Julian Cundiff **£9.99**

Other Best Sellers
Carp Sense by Jim Gibbinson **£14.95**

My Passion for Carp by Andy Little **£16.95**

Savay Lake by John Harry **£14.95**

Tiger Bay by Rob Maylin **£16.95**

In Pursuit of Carp and Catfish by Kevin Maddocks **£15.95**

☆ **COMING SOON** ☆
Two New Books From Kevin Maddocks
Euro Carp Fever & Euro Cat Fever
Watch Out For Them !

All these books can be purchased or ordered via your local tackle shop, if you find this not possible, you can obtain them direct from Beekay - simply add £2 per item for P+P

5. Natural Baits?

You'll notice I've placed a question mark after the sub-heading. It is there because the use of so-called natural baits is a subject I can get a bit hot under the collar about, but as this is a book about carp baits, it is a good arena in which to explain my views.

I am told that fishmeal boilies are natural. Not to me, they aren't, nor are they natural to a carp. So what exactly is a natural bait? Do they exist, in fact? I would argue that from a practical point of view, for the most part they do not. With the exception of mussels and bloodworm, I have never heard of any day to day food item that carp find in nature being a successful carp bait. Even mussels and bloodworm are not all that successful; certainly no more effective than a well made boilie.

Carp have very varied tastes as far as their choice of food is concerned. They eat scores of live animals such as bloodworms, snails, shrimps, daphnia, freshwater mussels and most of the other invertebrates which they encounter in vast quantities. They are quite capable of growing to a very large size by eating only purely natural food. However, it is also a fact that carp can and do grow very large indeed when fed a diet made up of such foodstuffs as pulses, nuts, seeds and boilies, none of which are in the least bit natural.

So is there any justification for using purely natural foods as bait for carp? Are they more effective or less so? Do they draw carp into a swim: do they trigger a feeding instinct? And what about the use of natural food in groundbait or as part of an overall bait comprising both natural and artificial foodstuffs?

I would argue that purely natural foods are nothing like as effective as boiled baits and I justify my contention by asking every one of you reading this to count the number of carp you have caught on mussels, crayfish, bloodworm, snails, freshwater shrimps and any of the host of other natural foods that occur naturally in most lakes, rivers and reservoirs. Done that? Now compare that with how many you have caught on artificial baits; case proved!

I fish an ancient estate lake which is wild and overgrown and very old. Some say it dates back to the 17th century. It has never been emptied or tampered with by the interferring hand of Man and the lake is full of natural food, particularly mussels, bloodworm, daphnia and shrimp. The lake is almost completely surrounded with towering old oak trees. The record for the lake is just over the thirty pound (13.6kg) mark.

For years the lake was very lightly fished and the carp were naive and comparatively easy to catch. Then, as angling pressure grew, they became more suspicious and as a result more advanced rigs and baits were needed to fool them.

In my early years on the lake, I found boiled baits were immediately effective, but nuts and pulse baits accounted for a greater number of fish. Over the years, properly applied fishmeal boiled baits supplied in quantity have put far more

24

fish on the bank than ever before. As a result the carp have grown more quickly than they ever did prior to the start of regular carp fishing on the lake in 1985 when only natural food was available to them. I believe this is proof that the carp in this particular lake have discovered that fishmeal boilies are nutritious and of overall benefit to their health, but how can anyone class fishmeals as a natural bait? What's natural about them?

The carp are usually caught at night and it is the practice to put them in a carp sack until the photo session in the morning. Many anglers have noted that as well as eating fishmeal boilies, at times the sacked fish had also been eating natural food prior to capture, usually small mussels, freshwater shrimp, bloodworm and at certain times of the year, acorns, either whole or crushed.

The presence of acorns is not unusual. There are, at times, thousands of them falling into the water off the surrounding oak trees and no doubt carp have become used to supplementing their diet with acorns, but nobody has ever caught a carp using an acorn as bait, and believe me, every angler who fishes the lake has tried them at some time or other.

And what about the small mussels? Again they've been tried and found somewhat ineffective. Does this prove that carp can be persuaded to eat artificial food almost to the exclusion of all other foods? I think it does.

Darenth Tip Lake was the site of a large scale experiment in the late 80s. A group of anglers agreed to bait the lake very heavily with fishmeal boilies. At one stage it was estimated that thousands of boiled baits a week were going into the small lake. You might imagine that such a massive amount of bait could never be eaten by the resident carp, but for about three years the lake fished like never before. Where one or two fish a trip was previously the average catch rate, this suddenly jumped to 8-10 in a 48-hour session, and the carp grew at an astonishing rate. Some very familiar fish that had never come anywhere near to 30lb (13.6kg) in weight, suddenly bolted past that weight and put on five, six, sometimes as much as ten pounds (4.5kg) in a summer!

I think that this proves what many on the lake thought at the time, that the carp were so preoccupied with eating artificial fishmeal boilies, that they actually stopped following their instinct to eat naturally occurring food.

It sometimes appears to me that in France there are more frogs per hectare than there are people, especially in the spring when they are being amorous and making the devil of a noise! As a result of all this heavy petting there must be countless millions of tadpoles in just about every French lake and pond during May and June and I am sure that carp often fill themselves with tadpoles from time to time. But how many of we carp anglers have actually tried using a tadpole as bait...and if you have, were you successful? I doubt it.

Finally let's look at crayfish as a natural bait. In England small river crayfish are without doubt the top bait for chub, but to the best of my knowledge I know of no authenticated captures of carp on crayfish baits....on crayfish flavouring or sense appeals, yes, definitely, but not on the real thing. Kingfisher Lake in Hampshire is home to some very big carp. It is also stiff with large crayfish. As you can imagine, the crayfish can be a pest to carp anglers by eating their baits, and many frustrated anglers have tried using crayfish tails and even whole crayfish as carp bait to try and keep other crayfish away from their hookbaits. As far as I know, not one has had a fish on them.

The same situation exists at the famous Withy Pool in Bedfordshire – the lake

CARP VIDEOS

Withy Pool: Carp Water Supreme - Kevin Maddocks	£13.99
Practical Carping 1: Julian Cundiff	£13.99
Practical Carping 2 : Julian Cundiff	£13.99
Practical Carping 3: Julian Cundiff	£13.99
Practical Carping 4: Julian Cundiff	£13.99
Big Carp Challenge 1: Mid-Northants - Alan Taylor	£13.99
Big Carp Challenge 2: Horton - Alan Taylor	£13.99
French Carping: An Introduction - Alan Taylor	£13.99
French Carping 1: River Seine - Marc Ponsot & Friends	£13.99
French Carping 2: Ton-Up, Lac Du Der - A. Taylor & Friends	£13.99
French Carping 3: Chantecoq Facts - A. Taylor & K. Maddocks	£13.99
French Carping 4: Big Carp - Orient - Kevin Maddocks	£13.99
French Carping 5: Successful Failure - P. Regent & K. Bishop	£13.99
Carp Fever 1: The Carp Revolution - Kevin Maddocks	£13.99
Carp Fever 2: Rigs & Baits - Kevin Maddocks	£13.99
Carp Fever 3: Bait & Rigs - Kevin Maddocks	£13.99
Carp Fever 4: Off the Top & Down Below - Kevin Maddocks	£13.99
Cold - Water Carping: Kevin Maddocks	£13.99
Italy: Basic Carping - Kevin Maddocks	£13.99
Italy: Advanced Carping - Kevin Maddocks	£13.99
Long Range Carping: Phil Hyde & Clive Gibbins	£13.99
Carp Teach-In: Andy Little & Friends	£13.99
Carp Fishing: (Cuttle Mill) - Des Taylor	£13.99
Stalking Carp: (On Floaters) - Des Taylor	£13.99
Euro Carp Quest 1: Fishabil - Kevin Maddocks	£13.99
Euro Carp Quest 2: Brive- Kevin Maddocks	£13.99

Best Sellers

Expedition Beluga: (Sturgeon To 273lb) - Kevin Maddocks	£13.99
Catfish Tour Of Europe: (Double Pack 2 x 60min)- K.Maddocks	£19.99
Big Cats Of The Volga: Kevin Maddocks	£13.99
Tench Fishing: David Maddocks	£13.99

All these videos can be purchased or ordered via your local tackle shop, if you find this not possible, you can obtain them direct from Beekay - simply add £2 per item for P+P

WITHY POOL, HENLOW CAMP, BEDFORDSHIRE. SG16 6EA.
Tel: 01462 816960
Fax: 01462 817253

is home to many thousands of crayfish and many visitors to the Pool have tried them as bait, but not a single carp has ever been caught on one.

Now all of the above is not to say that natural food is not important to us as carp anglers. On big waters your catch rate will almost certainly be governed by your ability to locate natural food larders. Carp are creatures of habit and they usually follow well defined patrol routes from one food source to another. The sight of carp jumping clear of the water may indicate a food larder on the lake bed below. Mussel beds are another place where it is wise to place your hookbait and free offerings. Deep silt often holds vast quantities of bloodworm and mussels, and I always search on marginal weed stems for freshwater snails. These natural foods are indicators that carp might be drawn to these areas to feed, and, given that I feel confident that my baits will often be preferred to natural foods, I am confident of successful fishing in or near natural food areas. So don't ignore these areas and use your skill at locating natural areas of food to locate feeding carp.

Extracts taken from natural food can be effective in both hookbaits and in groundbait. Fish are genetically programmed to eat zooplankton from the moment they hatch and carp will invariably investigate any source of zooplankton. Strangely, zooplankton stimulates the feeding instincts of a carp in much the same way as do some artificial flavours, attractors and stimulants that we use in carp baits. In fact, it is this reaction in carp that we are trying to trigger when we add such liquids and powders to our bait, their in-built natural reaction to feeding stimuli.

Many anglers refer to maggots, earthworms, bread, cheese and luncheon meat as natural baits, but they are no more natural than a fishmeal boilie. Carp are simply not accostomed to finding large quantities of maggots on the lake bed, nor do they often encounter earthworms, but both are fabulous carp baits. The same applies to brandlings, casters, luncheon meat and bread. They are not natural to the carp, but all are valid baits.

I have heard anglers refer to essential oils as natural. Natural in what respect? As far as a carp is concerned, there is nothing natural about essential oils and carp do not encounter them in their day to day life. The same applies to salt water marine extracts such as green lipped mussel extract, or fishmeals made out of mackerel, herring, sandeels, anchovy or any other type of sea dwelling creature.

Flavours are not natural to carp, not even the so-called nature-identical ones; nor are amino acid food complexes such as Minamino or Nutramino. True, they may mimic, to a certain degree, natural stimuli, but in and of themselves they are far from natural products. Betaine hydrochloride in the form I use it is nature identical, but it is not a true natural food. Again it mimics natural stimuli but in its crystalline form it is a synthetic product formed under laboratory conditions.

Therefore in the context of this contribution, I cannot accept any synthetic chemical, pulse, seed, worm, maggot, oil or any product that we add to boilies as "natural" in the true sense of the word. BUT, and it is a very big but, I VERY FIRMLY believe that we can use such products to our strong advantage to make baits that are 'BETTER THAN NATURE!'

I will not go on further about these so-called natural baits as I believe that there is more mileage to be had out of well made boiled baits than out of say, swan mussels or bloodworms.

6. Sweeteners and Colours

I don't know precisely who it was that first started using sweetened bait. I have a feeling it was the Richworth partners Clive Diedrich and Malcolm Winkworth who first began to use commercial, artificial sweeteners during their campaign on some of the hard pressured Surrey waters like Farnham AS water, Cut Mill. Particles and unsweetened boiled baits were the baits in vogue on most of the waters the pair fished and though they seemed to catch their share, it was obvious that the carp were ready for something new, so when Clive and Malcolm started baiting up with sweetened baits, the carp went crazy for them.

I am not sure which particular sweetener they used, but it may well have been a synthetic product such as liquid Hermesetas or any of the other saccharin-based products. Saccharin, like all the synthetic sweeteners, is widely used in the food and drinks industry to give a highly sweet taste without recourse to adding loads of natural sugars. Some feel that synthetic sweeteners have too much of an unnatural taste, but that is just us bestowing human characteristics on our quarry again. As far as carp are concerned, the primary attraction (smell) comes from the chemical make up of the synthetic product and the secondary attraction (taste) comes once the bait has been taken into the mouth and the taste buds have analysed the sweet taste. Exactly the same as with flavours, the combination of smell backed up by taste is what makes the sweetener an attractor in its own right.

I can recall when frozen ready-made baits first came onto the market. They were launched by the newly-formed Richworth company, the partners of which were Clive and Malcolm. Surely it was no coincidence that some of that early range was heavily sweetened. At the same time the company released a range of flavours and a bottled sweetener onto the market, so that those who preferred to make up their own baits could add a few of the Richworth secrets to their baits. These products, especially the sweetener, made an immediate impact on the bait scene and those in the know saw their catch rate soar overnight as they turned to the newly available flavours and the liquid sweetener.

In fact the overall success of all sweeteners should not come as any surprise. At a time when the majority of artificial flavours were based on very sharp, acidic chemicals, a product that could counter the bitter taste was bound to meet with considerable success. In the early days flavours came in for a great deal of abuse. It was not uncommon to hear of anglers adding 20-25ml of flavour to 500g of base mix.

Personally I am astonished that they caught at all, as at these levels unsweetened baits must have tasted awful. Sweeteners changed all that. By adding say, 5ml of liquid Hermesetas to the eggs, the acidic burn of the flavour disappeared to such a degree that it soon became fashionable to put as much as 30ml of flavouring in a pound mix. But when you raised the level of the flavour to such an extent, you

Ken looking happy with this cracking 40 pounder (18.2kg)

also needed to increase the amount of sweetener to counter the bitter taste. Mind you, for a while heavily sweetened baits carrying ridiculously high flavour levels were all the rage and the carp were mad for it.

The common opinion at that time was that there was no need for nutritious ingredients. The boilie was simply, "a carrier for the flavour" Yes! That's what was widely believed; that it was the flavour that caught the carp, not the base mix. As a result carp baits of the time were usually made up of low cost, poor quality ingredients. It was the high flavour level in combination with the effectiveness of the sweetener gave new life to an otherwise tired and jaded approach. The era of the 'crap' bait had well and truly arrived, thanks in no small part to sweeteners. I met several anglers during this period who were proud to refer to their base as an AOR Mix, the initials standing for, Any Old Rubbish! Fancy being proud about that!

Another peculiarity of most sweeteners is their alkaline pH. In effect this means that they help to counteract the acidic nature of most flavours by buffering the acid content with an alkaline one, thus raising the bait's pH up to a more tolerable level for the carp. However, it has to be remembered that most flavours are, in part at any rate, attractive precisely BECAUSE they are acidic, their attraction stemming from the localised pH change that we mentioned in the chapters on attraction. Any dilution of an acidic signal by an alkaline sweetener is likely to reduce the strength of the attraction of the flavour to some degree.

There are currently some very effective flavour/sweetener blends on the bait shelves. Sweet Nutraspice, Sweet Cream, Sweet Milk etc, These are very effective blends but to my mind you can't beat adding your own sweetener at the level you require it, not at the level the bait company wishes you to use it.

One of the best liquid sweeteners of all time has been Sweet Cajouser from

Nutrabaits. This intense sweetener has a lovely malty smell and taste so that as well as enhancing the flavour notes by adding sweetness, it also acts as a flavour in its own right. I know some anglers are using it at 5ml mto a 500g mix on its own to act as both flavour and sweetener.

Sweet powders are also very popular. The KM Perfector range of boosters, stimulants and enhancers included three powdered sweeteners; Intense Sweetener, Sweet Enhancer and Sweet Appetite Stimulator are handily packaged, low cost products designed to raise the flavour profile of your bait by enhancing the sweet note in the flavour.

One of the most effective was Cotswold Baits Milk B. Sadly Cotswold Baits are no longer trading, but I know that D.T. Baits can now offer exactly the same product under their own label. Another new sweetener is Nutrabaits' Creamy Super Sweet. This is probably one of the most intense sweeteners available, but it is not just a sweetener. The product has very pronounced cream and vanilla over-tones and these help to soften the taste of the sweetener to a large extent. In fact, Creamy Super Sweet could probably be used as a flavour/sweetener in its own right.

Powdered sweeteners work in much the same way as do liquid products but their advantage lies in the fact they they are much longer lasting within the bait. Being a powder they are generally less soluble and they are therefore less affected by water intake. Liquid sweeteners and flavours are much more soluble and as water breaks down the bait so the liquid content leaks out. There is therefore, a good argument for including both powdered and liquid sweeteners in your bait.

Most of these sweet products are highly concentrated and they usually have low recommended doseage levels. I would suggest that you stick to these rigidly, as to exceed them is to make your baits so sweet as to actually go beyond sweet-ness towards repulsiveness.

Of course, not all sweet products are synthetically produced. Natural sugars such as sucrose, glucose and fructose can all be used to sweeten a bait. Sucrose is the natural sugar obtained from sugar beet or sugar cane. It is, in effect, what you put in your tea! Glucose is probably one of the most widely occuring natural sugars and as such carp can readily recognise it. Fructose is actually a natural sugar obtained from various fruits. It is much more soluble than the other two sugars and ideal for sweetening the range of fruit flavours, rounding off the somewhat sharp edge that can occur with some synthetic fruit flavours.

Another range of chemicals that have a slightly sweet undertone includes glycerine and glycerol. Glycerol is a thick chemical product that is now being more widely used as a flavour base. This is due, in part, to its ability to counter any acidic aftertaste that may arise when the flavour itself is created. Though it is less soluble than pure sweeteners, glycerol is ideally suited to a wide range of flavour bases that may benefit from being slightly sweetened. Glycerol is also an emulsi-fier of oils, which makes blends of essential oils and glycerol-based flavours ideally suited to each other.

One truly excellent and totally natural sweetener is liquid molasses. It is used at much higher levels than artificial products – up to 15ml/500g – and is compati-ble with all types of base mix. Carp seem to find the smell of molasses highly stim-ulating, and though its taste is nothing like as extreme as an artificial product, it adds a significant, more natural balance to the all-round smell and taste of your baits. There was a time not too long ago when I seemed to be catching more common carp than previously. This coincided with a period when I was using a birdfood base mix with liquid molasses as the sweetener for the first time. Coincidence? I don't know. All I can tell you is that I'm not the first to notice this. If you've got a crafty common in your water that seldom makes a mistake, you could do a lot worse than to try liquid molasses.

There are, of course, a great many other sweet products that can be used in carp baits. Muscatel is a dark brown sugar that gives a very distinctive taste. It was one of the prime sweetening ingredients in the old soya/semolina recipes of the mid-80s. Icing sugar is yet another sucrose sugar that can be used to sweeten baits. Being finer and more highly refined, icing sugar blends superbly with most types of base mix. It also has the additional benefit of aiding the shelf life of a bait. That is not to say that it can be regarded as a pure preservative in the precise sense of the word, but a bait made with 15-20% (100g/500g) icing sugar will last twice as long as the same bait without the sugar. It is likely that high levels of icing sugar are used by the ready-made bait industry as part and parcel of the overall preserving proccess. Icing sugar should be dissolved in warmed flavour or liquid foods rather than in water. Adding water to any bait simply increases the risk of bacteria forming inside the bait, countering any preserving action the sugar may provide.

COLOURS IN CARP BAITS...WHY?

I have to say that I cannot see the logic of colouring a bait. As far as I am concerned, the bait's colour makes not the slightest difference! What is the point of trying to attract carp via their natural instincts and senses of taste and smell, only to risk scaring it off by adding some bright and gaudy colour that is not in the slightest bit natural. I tend to use baits that turn out pretty drab in colour anyway, but I am sure that on pressured waters, brightly coloured baits will be regarded as a danger sign by carp that have been caught a few times.

I suppose if you were fishing for virgin fish you could make a point for having very visible baits, but as virgin carp are practically a thing of the past these days, I can see more logic in using dull or dark baits to blend in with the bottom, rather than bright ones that draw attention to themselves and can soon become associated with danger.

The carp feeds primarily by using smell and taste. Sight is obviously significant, but only up to a point. There are plenty of examples of blind carp getting caught on anglers' baits, carp that have grown to a good size despite being unable to see and blind carp are certainly no easier to catch!

As far as I am concerned, bait colour is at best irrelevant, at worst a scare factor. If I were to consider colouring my baits, I would only do so to make them stand out less, not more. I suppose at the end of the day it's a confidence thing. As carp anglers we spend a great deal of time and money trying to make a carp bait as appealing to our quarry as we can in terms of its smell, taste and nutritional properties: if an angler feels that he needs to draw attention to his bait still further by making it stand out against the lake bed, well, why not. It's just not for me, that's all.

7. Proprietary Base Mixes

Perhaps you may feel that I have spent too many pages dealing with the subject of attraction, flavours and other attractors, but that is simply because I feel that in order to understand carp baits as a whole, it is very important to get to grips with all of the subject's component parts. It is no good having a dazzling and accurate grasp of attraction without backing this up with a thorough knowledge of food recognition, nutrition and digestion.

So having looked in general terms at the ways we can improve the attractiveness of our base mix, it is now time to look in greater detail at the mix itself.

The choice is wide and complex, but despite what the bait companies would have you believe, there is no such thing as an irresistible bait! The success of your season will not only depend on the right type of base mix for the water or waters you are fishing, but it will also rely heavily on your in-depth understanding of all aspects of the bait that you choose; how you apply it, when and where you introduce it and in what quantity. Your options and decisions will be governed by many factors, not least of which will be angling pressure and bait competition. The greater the choice of bait offered to the fish, the more you need to think about what you are offering, and why.

Then there are the natural cycles to consider; weather, atmospheric conditions, the presence – or lack of it – of natural food in the lake, and so on. In order to make sure you are on the right base mix at the right time, we must look in detail at the various types of mix currently available.

I suppose when you boil it all down to basics, there are really only four types of carp bait mix. All provide a form of nutrition to a greater or lesser degree, and all will catch on a long term basis, provided that the attractors are used at a long term level rather than for an instant hit.

Top of the tree are base mixes formed by mixing a combination of very high quality, 80-90% pure protein ingredients. These ingredients are usually based upon the pure proteins of milk, eggs, soya and whey. Over the years these baits have come to be known as HNV baits, or baits with a high nutritional value. However, this definition has now broadened to include most mixes with an effective balance of nutrition such as the more sophisticated fishmeal and birdfood mixes, so perhaps for our purposes it is better to refer to these very refined and expensive mixes as High Protein base mixes. Typical examples of these mixes are Hi-Nu-Val from the Nutrabaits range, or the HpNV Compound from the Kevin Maddocks Bait range. The initials stand for High Palatability & Nutritional Value.

A very popular type of mix in recent years has been the fishmeal base mix, examples of which include Nutrabaits' Big Fish Mix and Fishfood Mix, and the Fishmeal Blend from the KM stable. Other highly effective fishmeal mixes are The S Mix from Nash Baits and Premier's Fish Mix. As their names imply, the princi-

pal ingredients used in these bases are fishmeals, but the examples quoted above
are not simply a rag-bag mix of various meals with a crude binder to keep the
sticky mess together. The most effective fishmeal base mixes also include a range
of other products, including a proportion of refined pure proteins, in order to give
the overall mix a more balanced nutritional package.

Then there are the mixes that are formulated with a selection of commercial
foodstuffs generally intended for use as bird feeds. These baits are called, naturally enough, birdfood mixes. They differ from high protein and fishmeal bases in
that they are generally lower in protein but much higher in fats and carbohydrates.
In an ideal world carp derive the majority of their energy from fats, so it has
become common to see birdfood base mixes refered to as High Fat or High Energy
baits.

About now you are saying to yourself, "This is getting complicated!" but all
you have to remember is that each type of bait has its advantages and disadvantages and as these pages unfold I hope you will be able to see the differences
between the various baits and be able to work out in your own mind, how, when
and where to use them.

So to recap: so far we have seen that the three main types of base mix that
can supply or supplement the carp's diet are High Protein baits made of milk, egg
and soya proteins, sophisticated blends of fishmeals and other ingredients to give
a high nutritional value, and birdfood baits which are also nutritional but in a different way, namely by supplying fats which can be converted into energy by the
carp; the so-called High Energy bait. It has become common these days to refer to
all of the above as FOOD BAITS and that is a pretty accurate description of them.
The term suggests that if introduced in a reasonable quantity they can supply a
necessary part of the carp's everyday diet, and with proper application and dedi-

Trout pellets – the basis for many 'Specials'.

cation on the angler's part, carp will come to search for these types of bait, in preference to others, knowing that they are actually a beneficial part of their day to day food requirements. Once that situation has been achieved, catching carp becomes a whole heap easier!

There is a fourth type of bait which is of lower food value and thus cannot truly be classed as a pure food bait. These are the so-called 50/50 mixes also sometimes rather crudely referred to as 'crap' baits. They are generally of a much lower nutritional worth and they rely to a large extent on the strength of the attractors and other additives to draw carp into the swim. However, it would be wrong of you to regard them as simply carriers for a food signal. This was the case in the early 80s when heavily sweetened baits with extremely high flavour levels, based on junk ingredients, were in vogue. In fact, 50/50 mixes are just another weapon in the bait armoury and if they are correctly put together and properly applied they can be effective over a reasonably long period. However, they will not have the year-on-year effectiveness of pure food baits that are properly applied.

We've looked in detail at the nature of attraction, but it must be remembered that it is not the flavours and other additives that make a long term food bait, it is the base mix. We add flavours and attractors to a long term food base in order to give the bait a recognisable label that fish will come to recognise as indicating the presence of food. If, at the same time, this label is also an attractor (in the case of a flavour), or even a food in its own right (as is the case with liquid food additives such as Multimino), then so much the better. The label has now become the attractor and you have the best of both worlds.

As we've seen from the sections on attraction it is quite possible to take a top quality food bait and turn it into an straightforward attractor bait simply by increasing the level at which you use the additives. Alternatively, you can offer a bait with a comparatively low food value, but if the attractors are applied at lower long term levels, and the flavour is backed up with say 30ml/500g of a liquid food additive, then even a 50/50 mix can have a long catching life. So it is important to look at the concept of food baits in conjunction with attractive additives in order to understand the role that each plays in establishing your bait as something the carp enjoys feeding upon.

But in order to get a more in-depth insight into the various alternative mixes, it is necessary to pop back in time to a point when carp fishing as we know and understand it was in its infancy.

Once upon a time there was no such thing as a proprietary base mix for carp baits. When I was "cutting my carp fishing teeth" on Keston Ponds (and failing miserably), Big Fish Mix was two decades away from being launched, Kevin Nash was probably just learning how to catch roach from the local canal, Bill Cottam was still in nappies (what an awesome thought) and Kevin Maddocks was still a few years away from managing a rock 'n roll super group that stopped just short of actually becoming super. Mind you, Tim Paisley was an old man at the time and he's not getting any younger!

It was the mid-60s and simple paste baits were the order of the day. Often the basic ingredient was some kind of pet food such as Kit-E-Kat cat food mixed with breadcrumbs and maybe flour to hold the messy goo together while you cast out. Another popular ingredient was a tin of mashed sardines which was added to the binder. Two other very popular ingredients were sausage meat and luncheon meat. The meat, fish, cat food or whatever made up about 50% of the total weight of the mix, the rest comprised some sort of binder or stiffener. As before, this was often no more than ordinary breadcrumbs, but these were later replaced by match anglers groundbaits such as Pomenteg. Later, even better binders such as wheat gluten were used.

One of the better bases was ground trout pellets. What's that? You think they are a new development? They've been around almost as long as modern carp fishing has! There's nothing new in trout pellets; even thirty years ago the pellets were doing the business.

The main problem with these baits is that EVERYTHING liked them, not just carp. Soft pastes were soon whittled away by bream and roach and a carp had to be quick off the mark if it wanted a mouthful before the paste was all gone. But therein lay the problem, for carp were as wary then as they are now, and their natural caution made them suspicious of these nice smelling but somewhat unnatural offerings that other coarse fish found so instantly appetising. What was needed was a way to keep the paste intact on the lake bed for a longer period so as to give carp time to overcome its caution and begin feeding on the free offerings.

Early boiled baits were known in fact as skinned baits. They were made of the same basic pet food ingredients but this time eggs and flour or wheat gluten was added to the mix so that by rolling the paste into balls and dropping them into boiling water a hard outer skin was formed which would prevent nuisance fish from whittling away at the paste. The boilie was born but at this stage in their development these baits were not referred to as such. In fact, even once the term found limited favour, the true ultra-cult boys would never refer to their baits as 'boilies'! You were on boiled baits, mate!

As in all walks of life, early development lead to more and more refinement. By the late-60s and early-70s the word "Specials" was being whispered on the grapevine. Everybody had their own thoughts on what comprised a special bait; some were a great deal more special than others, which were in effect little more than glorified boiled catfood pastes. But in a select few kitchens the first purpose-made carp food was being formulated.

I suppose these early baits would be regarded as pretty simple base mixes by today's standards, but for the first time anglers began thinking about the food aspect of their baits and the key element became the bait's nutritional balance. Trout pellets, PYM (Phillip's Yeast Mixture), Wheatgerm, Equivite, Codlivine, casein, and wheat gluten were the key ingredients, but there was a great deal of ignorance about how to use and apply these products. It was often a case of the blind leading the blind and many turned away from the better bait ingredients when they couldn't get them to work as they were supposed to. Meanwhile the thinkers continued to refine their use still further and stretched ahead in the carp catching stakes. Kent angler Fred Wilton is rightly credited with being the first angler to conceive the idea of a balanced nutritional bait. He argued that a carp will come to recognise an artificial food source in fullfilling part and parcel of its everyday food, but only if that food source is formulated in such a way as to provide all the carp's nutritional requirements in one go. At the same time, it follows that the entire bait, not just parts of it, should be as digestible as possible.

Today the Wilton principle is widely accepted as the foundation of modern carp baits and Fred as the founding father of all subsequent developments. We all owe him a debt of gratitude for his pioneering work. No doubt if Fred hadn't come along when he did, somebody else would eventually have stumbled down the same road, but Fred was the first and arguably is still the best when it comes to original thinking. It is thanks to him that the carp bait shelves in tackle shops the length and breadth of the country are piled high with all manner of base mixes, flavours and other attractors. The proliferation of bait companies must astonish Fred, and it also still manages to amaze and confound the doomsayers in the trade who said it would never last!

Despite many protestations to the contrary from the bait companies, all the various types of base mix comprise many of the same few basic ingredients, albeit in widely varying proportions. As an example let us look at the various types of mix in a bit more detail

Undoubtedly fishmeal base mixes have been the success story of the late 80's and have continued their rise throughout the 90's. I wouldn't be at all surprised if at least 75% of all carp caught in the UK these days don't fall for the temptations offered by a fishmeal boilie. One of the first true fishmeal base mixes was Rod Hutchinson's Seafood Blend. This was really the only fishmeal base mix then available until the arrival of the Kent-based Premier Baits company. Their original base mixes, when used in conjunction with high levels of Omega-3 fatty acid fish oils, were to revolutionise the science of carp baits. Nowadays every major bait manufacturer includes at least one fishmeal-based mix in their range.

However, the original concept of a fishmeal bait has been refined and taken to extremes that the original prototypes could never hope to emulate. You see, single fishmeals on their own proved not nearly as satisfactory as a blend of fish-meals and birdfood ingredients. Some bait firms have even added top quality milk proteins to their mix. One such blend comprising all three basic ingredients is Nutrabaits Big Fish Mix. This contains the blend of fishmeals together with added birdfoods – Sluis CLO and Robin Red – along with the pure proteins, acid casein and Nutrapro (an isolated whey protein). The mix is crowned with the addition of kelp powder and a vitamin and mineral supplement; as you can see, a complete and balanced food mix that supplies all that a carp needs by way of nutrition. This is probably one of the most effective mixes of all time. It was developed by Dave Moore, an extremely experienced and respected angler and when Dave puts a bait together for you, you'd be a fool not to use it!

Birdfood baits are often confused with seed baits. This is not the case. OK, birdfoods do contain a fair proportion of seeds, but not all seeds make good carp baits. Some of the most successful birdfood ingredients come from the Cleethorpes-based company J.E. Haith & Son, a name that you will hear a great deal more of in the sections on birdfoods, particles, seeds and other types of carp bait.

Birdfood baits work in a different way from fishmeals, but both are similar in two significant respects. The first is that their coarse textures allow water to pene-trate quickly and easily to the heart of the bait. This in turn forces the flavours and other additives in the bait to seep into the lake water surrounding the bait carpet, thus acting as an attractor package that the carp will hopefully investigate. Secondly, they are both highly digestible and break down fairly quickly once intro-duced to the lake.

Birdfoods differ from fishmeals in one important respect; they are generally higher in fat and lower in protein than fishmeals. (Remember we referred to them as High Energy baits earlier on?). As we will see later on in the book both need to be applied in a different fashion in order to get the best from them. For the time

being, if you just remember that fat equals energy as far as a carp is concerned and there are times when energy is a prime requirement in our quarry and other times when it is not as vital; when protein becomes more important. We'll go into this aspect of bait application a little later on.

Milk, egg and whey protein baits – the High Protein baits – are still the bait of choice for many of today's top carp anglers. These days, this type of bait is rather out of favour, perhaps due to the high cost. Indeed, right from the start of the High Protein experiments such baits have attracted their fair share of criticism, but there is no getting over the fact that loads and loads of carp all over the country still get caught on highly refined 90% pure protein-based baits.

Typical ingredients that go to make up a high protein base mix include both acid and rennet casein, calcium and sodium caseinate, lactalbumin, lactoglobulin, isolated whey protein, egg albumin and soya isolate. Using these ingredients it is possible to formulate a base mix which, even after it is mixed with eggs, will still have a very high protein content.

A lot of thinking has gone into the formulation of modern high protein base mixes. I think we all now accept that in the past, baits with an excessive protein level were not digested properly with the result that much of the goodness of the protein was wasted. However, some of the real heavy dudes in the bait world such as Tim Paisley and Keith Sykes started to venture down a different road. They theorised that by using specific protein-digesting enzymes the high protein content of these kinds of baits could be made more digestible, while others argued that by lowering the proportion of the very high protein ingredients, and blending them on a more digestible base, the carp would be able to utilise the protein content to its full extent.

I have been down both roads and believe that both have their merits. My experiments with enzyme baits provided me with some of the most exciting fishing I've ever experienced. It was a case, literally, of "don't put the rod down!" But enzymes are notoriously hard to work with and at times laboratory conditions are needed in order to trigger the necessary effect. That said, if you are prepared to go for it, I still reckon that some form of enzyme treatment is the route to follow.

As far as I know there are only two bait firms that offer enzymes and enzymes-based products. Nutrabaits' Addit Digest is an excellent mixture of various enzymes specifically designed to work on milk proteins. The idea of the Addit Digest is to trigger a chemical reaction WITHIN THE BAIT ITSELF that would not only make a much higher proportion of the protein available for digestion but would also – and this is equally as important – allow the locked-in food signal to escape from the bait, flooding the lake water with a tantalising, almost irresistible smell and taste of top quality food. The other enzyme-based product is the KM Enzyme Assister, from the KM Bait Perfector range, which is a similar product that is intended to assist in breaking down the complex proteins into more easily digestible compounds.

The use of enzymes is something of a grey area for many anglers: sometimes they work brilliantly, others...? It's a complicated business, hit and miss at times, expensive, frustrating and often a complete waste of time...but every now and then, watch out!

Finally we come to the virtually protein-free, high carbohydrate base mixes that follow the so-called 50/50 principle. This classification was originally applied to Richworth's 50/50 mix, a blend of semolina, soya flour and other low protein ingredients that set the standard for many similar mixes that have followed. It was once quite popular to decry these types of base mix as rubbish or 'crap' baits, but recent thinking in the bait world now accepts that this label is unfounded.

Cheap base mixes can and do provide an excellent alternative to high protein baits, and far from just being a carrier for the smell, which is how they were once widely regarded, properly applied 50/50 mixes are among the most successful carp baits.

So that has given you a basic overall summary as far as base mixes are concerned. Now it is time to get right under the skin of the various types of mix and we'll kick off with the most important development of the past decade – fishmeals.

8. Fishmeals

I would guess that only the complete newcomer to carp fishing will have missed the fact that fishmeal baits have been the 'in' bait over the past decade or so, and even a comparative novice will probably not need me to tell him just how effective such baits have been in recent years.

Yes, fishmeals have arrived with a bang and now it seems you can hardly pick up the weeklies without seeing copious proof that yet again, some of the biggest fish in the UK and abroad have fallen to baits of this type. I suppose most readers will assume that fishmeals simply arrived out of the blue in the late 80s when Premier Baits first brought their use to the attention of the carp angling public, but in fact, fishmeals have been around for a lot longer than that.

In theory I suppose you could look to the 60s and 70s – when ground fish pastes, trout pellets and tinned fish were first used as the basis for carp baits – for the origin of fishmeal baits. However, the first true carp baits based on fishmeals was Rod Hutchinson's Seafood Blend. This pungent orange-coloured mix hit the market in about 1980 and was very effective, but at the time I don't think the great angling public was quite ready for the advances in bait technology that Seafood Blend represented. However, a select few in the know soon realised that fishmeals made very effective carp baits, and that properly applied they would out-fish most other baits hands down.

Several bait dealers played with the idea but few managed to get a satisfactory mix that would not only catch fish but would also bind together properly and roll out well on a bait roller. Most of the early experimental mixes were a nightmare to roll, and finding a binder that worked efficiently was a real struggle. Wheat gluten worked, after a fashion, but it wasn't really satisfactory. I think that a great many of us who dabbled with fishmeals in the early days got fed up with the many failures and went back to baits we knew would roll, bind and catch.

In addition, the early fishmeals also had a tendency to float which was not too useful! However, in time more refined fishmeals became available and some anglers began experimenting yet again, this time with some of the more sticky birdfoods such as Sluis CLO and Red Band canary food in combination with fishmeals. These were more effective binders than the old gluten and semolina alternatives and after a lot of hard work one company in particular came up with a red hot bait that rolled well, boiled hard and caught fish.

The Kent based company Premier Baits hit the headlines with some staggering catches from all over the UK on their own unique fishmeal recipe and that is when the carp angling public sat up and began to take notice. By the early 90's there was hardly a water in the land that had not been Prem'd and fishmeals were with us to stay. Soon every bait company had at least one fishmeal base mix in its list and as better and better ingredients were discovered, so the whole principle

Lots of fishmeals ready for a session on a French lake.

was refined and made more effective by the addition of fish oils and liquid foods.

So what exactly are fishmeals, how do they work, and why are they so effective? Fishmeals stand out first and foremost because of their digestibility. Carp seem to find them a doddle to eat and to pass through their digestive system to maximum effect. The metabolic process of converting food into energy is probably more effective with fishmeals than with any other type of bait. In addition they have a unique and highly identifiable smell that is almost instantly recognised as food by the carp. Their unique smell seems to become so imprinted on the carp's brain that it is almost impossible for the bait to blow. Quite simply carp adore them and will eat them by the bucketful.

You can catch carp on fishmeals without any further additives, flavours or attractors, though obviously, the more attractive you can make a bait, the more effective it will be. That said, I have caught a huge number of big carp on Big Fish Mix taken straight from the bag with no extra additions whatsoever, either in liquid or in powder form.

Fishmeals are not regarded by some anglers as pure protein ingredients, and certainly when compared to something like rennet casein which has a 95% protein value, white fish meal at 65% protein seems to fall well behind in terms of nutrition, but bear in mind that carp cannot adequately use all of the casein's 95% protein so you are losing nothing by dropping down the scale a bit. In addition rennet casein, while high in pure protein, is not as nutritionally balanced as white fish meal which is a much more acceptable food. Fishmeals are generally quite high in fat – remember what we said before about fat being important to carp as an energy source? – and this factor combined with a protein level of 60% or higher allows the carp to use the built-in fat content to provide their energy, while the protein can be used for tissue repair, growth and improvement in overall condition. As you can see, there is a high degree of digestibility with very little wastage where fishmeal baits are concerned.

Another huge advantage of fishmeals is that they are usually an almost instant success on most waters. Carp seem to accept them straight away, and it is fair to say that carp will eat huge quantities of fishmeals, provided you have not gone too silly on the attractors and flavours.

Fishmeals are generally coarse ground powders. This allows the lake water to penetrate the bait with ease, so forcing out the natural oils that are inherent in most fishmeals. As the oil is forced out, it attracts carp that are drawn by its smell. At the same time, as the bait takes on lake water, the bait begins to break down, as bacteria in the lake water goes to work on the ingredients. This breakdown is yet another major advantage of fishmeals. It's virtually impossible for uneaten fishmeals to remain so for long. Even if a carp does not eat the bait as it breaks down, it is quite probable that, as the bait softens small fish will be able to attack it. When fishing over fishmeal baits, it is a massive advantage knowing that you are fishing over a carpet of comparatively fresh bait all the time.

Fishmeals come in many different grades depending on the use to which they are going to be put. Some very indifferent fishmeals are used as fertilisers. These are usually multi-species meals comprising fish bones, heads and scraps of flesh left on the skeleton after filleting, real bottom of the barrel stuff. In the long distant past this meal was actually used as the basis of one or two carp baits, but as far as I know they are not used today by any bait firm as better, more refined meals have now become much more widely available.

White fish meal is the most popular feed meal. It is used in trout and other fish pellets, pig and chicken feeds and of course, in carp base mixes. It is made of the bones and scraps of skin and flesh left behind after white fish (cod, whiting, haddock, ling and some flatfish) have been proccessed. High in protein, high in oil content, it is a first class bait ingredient that can be used to form the bulk of most fish meal baits. Its main drawback is the high oil content which sometimes makes a base mix using a high proportion of white fish meal bound with, say, wheat gluten, very hard to roll. Better binders and more refined fish meals have nowadays led to easy-to-roll, easy-to-bind fishmeal mixes that will boil hard in 90 seconds.

Other fish meals are made by processing the entire fish, dehydrating the result, and grinding to powder form. These too are used almost exclusively as feeds. Sandeel, capelin, anchovy, whitebait, squid, crab and sardine are some of the most common meals. Unfortunately the ever-increasing technology used by industrial commercial fishing boats means that many species are in danger of being wiped out. The capelin is one such species.

Fishmeals on their own will not stick together and need a binder of some kind. Ordinary breadcrumbs are used in some mixes but this is a pretty inferior product. One of the best binders is a bird feed called Sluis CLO. By adding 3oz (75g) of Sluis to 6oz (150g) of mixed fishmeals a useful base for a carp bait can be formed. Finish the mix off with vitamins and minerals and a touch of either acid or rennet casein and a specialist binder such as Nutragel (from Nutrabaits) and you arrive at an excellent bait.

A typical recipe might be as follows:
200g mixed fishmeals
100g Sluis CLO
75g Nutragel
75g rennet casein
50g vitamin and mineral supplement.

To this you might think you would need to add flavours and other attractors, but while these will certainly help, they are by no means essential. I was one of the last guys in my region to switch to fishmeals but I was lucky to be the first angler to use an unflavoured version at Salamander Lake where I enjoyed considerable success on a similar recipe to the one shown above. You can be confident that a good fishmeal base mix will catch carp on its own, without the need for other additives. This is due to its inherent smell and its taste, not forgetting its in-built natural oil content, an excellent attractor in its own right.

There is no doubting the fact that carp find fishmeals very attractive. I feel confident in stating that a top quality fishmeal bait, properly applied with low levels of attractors would keep catching more or less indefinitely. As an effective food bait it has no equals. As an example let me use College Reservoir, a 40-acre water near my home in Cornwall.

This lake was one of the first to be blitzed by a hit squad from Premier Baits and from 1986 – 1990 baiting teams using Premier's fishmeals really bagged up on the water. If you weren't on fishmeals during this period, you simply did not catch. For some reason fishmeals fell from grace at the water and ready mades became all the rage for a time. "You gotta get on the readies," said the guys who were catching. "Fishmeals are finished!"

They were wrong, as the more experienced anglers on the lake knew they would be. Even the best ready-mades will never be able to compete ON A LONG TERM BASIS, and you simply cannot keep a good bait down for long, particularly when the competing bait is of comparatively low food value. Fishmeals are once again the most effective bait on College; they catch loads of carp and will continue to do so in the years to come.

Having said earlier that fishmeals have a naturally balanced food value, it would be wrong for you to think of them as in any way natural in themselves. Let's face it, fishmeals based on salt water species are as alien in fresh water as are bird feeds. However, they attract and keep on attracting because of their overall nutritional properties of high fat content, excellent palatability and, most importantly, their superb digestibility. It is this last aspect that sets them apart. Once a water has seen fishmeals, they will keep on working almost indefinitely, and only ridiculously excessive flavour levels could possibly cause a short-term blow-out.

And believe me, the blow-out WILL only be short-term, for exactly the reason I mentioned earlier, namely their fast breakdown rate. Most fishmeal baits will go soft after 24-36 hours in the water and break down to a mush within 72 hours. By the time they have broken down to this degree, even a ludicrously overloaded flavour level will have washed out of the bait and the mush becomes palatable once again. So even an angler who has been rather over-zealous in his flavour level is likely only to suffer in the short term. Once the temporary repulsion effect he has created gradually seeps out of the bait until a more tolerable, and more attractive level is reached, the carp and other fish will soon come back for a feed.

Some fishmeals are cheap and cheerful and only reasonably effective, some are cheap, not at all cheerful and not effective at all, and some are the bee's knees. The mixes that have stood the test of time are undoubtedly those with an overall balance of foodstuffs that complement the fishmeal base. I make no bones about it, if I was forced to make a choice of one bait that I had to stick too for life, it would be Nutrabaits Big Fish Mix. Runner-up would be the Nash Baits S Mix. There are others that are perhaps as good, but these two have proved themselves over and over again in my opinion.

No mention of fishmeals would be complete without looking at the use of fish oils as an attractor. It is not taking anything away from Premier's base mixes to say that a lot of their success was down to the use of high levels of fish oils. A level of 30ml to a half-kilo was commonly used. At first no problems seemed apparent, but once the majority of anglers on a lake started piling oil-laced baits into the water, the carp began to show signs of obesity, with all the problems that brings. After a few years the corpses of big fat carp with oil saturated blood and livers were found at waters throughout the country. Rightly or wrongly, the high levels of oils in fishmeal baits has been blamed for this and nowadays the excessive use of fish and other oils is not encouraged.

Though fish oils are an extremely effective additive and attractor they should be used responsibly. I'd suggest a level no higher than 10ml/500g but I know others would take issue with this saying that is just too low. Personally I prefer to err on the side of caution rather than on the side of my ego. I may catch more fish on fishmeals with excessive oil levels, but I may also be slowly killing my quarry; a rather blinkered attitude if you ask me.

Rather than add large quantities of oil to the bait itself, I prefer to use them as a soak. You can add neat fish oil to the finished baits at the rate of 10ml to a completed mix of bait for added attraction. This should be poured over the cold baits which have been placed in a polythene bag. Freezing the baits at this stage helps draw the oil into the bait. This 'outside' oil is meant to form a trickle of tiny oil droplets from the bait to the surface, acting as an attractor. The 'inside' oil will also leak out as the bait breaks down, but will do so much more slowly. If the bait is eaten within 2-3 hours of being introduced most of the 'outside' oil will have become detached from the bait and will not pose a threat to the carp. The small amount of 'inside' oil will be digested by the carp and used as a fat source.

A major problem with all fish oils is their tendency to go rancid. This is due to a process known as oxidisation. A simple remedy has been to add anti-oxidants to the oil at the bottling stage which effectively stops fish oils from going rancid.

Nutrabaits is one bait firm that adds such anti-oxidants to all their oils.

Many fish oils thicken considerably in cold weather, but there are some that do not react to low temperatures in this way, and as such they are ideal for winter use. These include, Salmon Oil, Blended Fish Oil, Winterised Pilchard Oil and the Complete Food Oil (from Nutrabaits).

Most of the top quality fishmeal base mixes actually comprise only about one third fishmeals, for it has been found that a blend of fishmeals, birdfoods and milk and egg proteins is a more effective bait than one with a higher level of fishmeals in it. The Big Fish Mix, for instance contains three fishmeals, two birdfoods, three milk proteins a vitamin and mineral supplement, and powdered kelp to add even further to its nutritional properties. If you add 2grams each of Betaine HCl and Green Lipped Mussel Extract to that little lot, you will have a bait that is second to none.

Here is my favourite recipe based on Big Fish Mix.

500g BFM
20ml Multimino-PPC
2g Betaine – dissolved in the Multimino-PPC.
2g Green Lipped Mussel Extract.
8ml Nutrabaits' Caviar UTCS.
3ml Cranberry Nutrafruit
1ml Sweet Cajouser
12 drops Black Pepper essential oil
20ml Multimino-PPC
10ml Salmon Oil.

An alternative attractor package would be:
6ml Tutti-Fruiti
20ml Nutramino
1ml Sweet Cajouser
15ml Complete Food Oil (Nutrabaits).

I would put that bait, with either of those attractor packages, up against any other recipe in the land. My friends and I have caught so many fish on them we have literally lost count, so I suggest that you at least give it a try. Surely those Big Fish Mix captures from around the country can't all be coincidence!

The NEW range of Kevin Maddocks carp attractors.

KM Boilies

The Kevin Maddocks range of shelf-life boilies were the very first to become popular in the U.K. and Europe. Our many years of producing ready-mades is only too clear when you pick up a packet – perfect shape, colour, texture, smell and taste. And most importantly - they catch a lot of fish too. Kevin Maddocks uses them on every trip at home and abroad and he wouldn't do that unless they were brilliant! They are available in 10mm Minis, 15mm Standards, 20mm Professionals and 25mm Donkey Chokers. The 10mm Minis are available in 200g packs at £3.99, the 15mm Standards are available in 200g Handy packs at £3.50 and 400g at £4.99. Professional packs cost £9.99 and are available in 15 or 20mm. For the price conscious angler and those travelling to other countries - 5kg Session carrier bag at £29.99 or a 10kg Euro carrier bag at £59.99. For full range of flavours see Boilie Flavours list.

KM Pop-Ups

The KM Pop-Ups have been on the market long enough now to be of the perfect quality - and that they are! Each pack contains 50 Pop-Ups and these are mixed in 15 and 20mm sizes. They are available in the ten KM Boilie flavours, plus the ever-popular Neutral (no flavour), so you can glug, spray or soak them in our range of Hookbait Enhancers or your very own exclusive flavours.

Price £3.99 a pack. For a full range of flavours see Boilie Flavours list.

KM Bait Perfector Sachets

A revolutionary range of 20 high-tech powder additives for carp anglers that strive to produce their own ultimate bait. The majority of the range consists of extremely high quality palatants, enhancers and stimulators which have been produced for us by technicians in one of Europe's finest laboratories. Each additive is carefully packed in totally encapsulated sachets at the source of production to ensure complete and essential freshness and recommended dosages are shown on the reverse of each sachet. A further information sheet is also available.

Price 99p per sachet

KM Base Mixes

1kg	Boilie Mix	£4.99
1kg	Bird Food Blend	£5.99
1kg	Fishmeal Blend	£5.99
1kg	H.p.N.V. Compound	£6.99
2.5kg	50/50 Boilie Mix	£8.99

KM Bait Perfector Liquid Flavours

This range of flavours is well proven and contains our most famous and successful flavours, such as the legendary Cream RM30 and Honey Syrup. The range is available in glass bottles (like all good flavours should be) in 30ml and 100ml. Flavours include: Strawberry Crush, Sweet Milk, Tutti Frutti, Clockwork Orange, Freshwater Crayfish, Sweet Corn, Choco Mint, Honey Syrup and Cream RM 30.
Prices are £2.49 and £5.99 respectively.

THE CUSTOMERS COME FIRST

Don't be fobbed off with inferior boilies just because that's all your dealer has in stock! He can easily place a phone order with us and have the bait in a few days.
If you encounter difficulties, report this to us on 01462 816960 and we will make sure you get the bait you want.

KM Donkey Chokers™

Want to catch the bigger fish? Then KM Donkey Chokers™ could be the answer to your dreams. Each pack contains 40 hand-made, specially hardened 25mm hookbaits. If you are fishing heavily stocked waters where the smaller fish get to the bait first, these Donkey Chokers™ will put off 'nuisance' fish and the smaller carp. They are also the perfect bait for french carp fishing. Available in packs of floaters (pop-ups) or sinkers.

Price: £4.99 a pack.

For full range of flavours see Boilie Flavours list.

KM Snowman™

The Snowman™ hookbait presentation is the latest alternative to standard boilie fishing and works extremely well on most waters. The new KM Snowman™ packs contain 50 specially-made boilies, half of which are floaters and half sinkers. One of each are fished on a hair, the sinker being nearest the hook. The buoyancy of the floating boilie takes the weight of the sinker so that they gently rest on the bottom. No shot or putty is required. The weightless Snowman™ is easily sucked in and is often taken before any free offerings are picked up. Available in 15mm or 20mm.

Price: £3.99 a pack.

For full range of flavours see Boilie Flavours list.

KM Boilie Flavours

Strawberry Oil Palatant\	Rosehip XL	Monster Mussel
Honey Necta	Tutti Frutti	Neutral (No flavour)
Peach Oil Palatant	Indian Spice	Squidmeal X Mix
Ultra Birdspice	Cream RM30	

New flavours in the KM boilie range this year are: Rosehip XL, Indian Spice, Monster Mussel, and Peach Oil Palatant. The very successful Wild Strawberry has now been blended with our new liquid palatant and is re-named: Strawberry Oil Palatant. Squidmeal has been further improved with our liquid smell and is now re-named: Squidmeal X Mix.

Following the success of our neutral pop-ups, the complete KM boilie range is now available in neutral (no flavour). You can simply soak, spray or glug them with your favourite flavour; your own exclusive bait without the hassle of making boilies!

Donkey Chokers™, Liquid Smells™, Snowman™, Bait Perfectors™ and Cream RM30™ are registered Trade marks belonging to Beekay International.

KM Hookbait Enhancer Dips

The KM Hookbait Dips were the first on the market. Not only are they the most successful in terms of sales but they are also the most effective. This year we have improved them even further with the addition of our new liquid palatant and the new flavours to match our boilie range.

150ml of liquid in a 250ml tub: £4.99.

KM Liquid Smells™

The new KM Liquid Smells™ are probably the only flavours ever developed solely for carp fishing use (the majority being food-grade flavours simply re-packed). From inception to perfection, the emphasis on these fluids has been HIGH in smell, LOW in taste. The high smell ensures that carp detect your bait more easily, especially during the night or when they are at distance. The low taste ensures immediate acceptance as soon as the carp

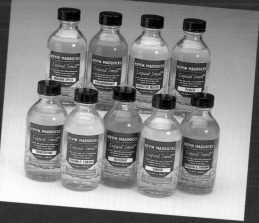

samples your bait. These new Liquid Smells™ represent a major step forward in the development of carp attractors. Make sure you get a slice of the action! Available in Strawberry, Peach, Rosehip, Squid, Indian Spice, Monster Mussel, Tangerine, Prawn & Shrimp, Double Cream
Price: £9.99 per 100ml glass bottle.

Quality Counts

We should like to point out, that we make no apologies for our boilies not being the cheapest on the market - it is a proven fact that high quality boilies catch more fish (and promote healthy growth) and we take pride in the fact that our boilies are of the very highest quality possible.

BEEKAY INTERNATIONAL

Withy Pool, Henlow Camp, Bedfordshire SG16 6EA. Tel: 01462 816960 Fax: 01462 81725

9. Birdfoods

I suppose that birdfood baits are probably one of the most widely used carp baits in current use. They are usually comparatively cheap, highly digestible and very attractive to carp. In the early days many anglers made a mix by simply adding wheat gluten to a combination of two or three birdfoods and dosing the whole shebang with a heavy glug of flavour and sweetener. Amazingly these baits worked, but only for a short time.

Early birdfood baits used the high attract principle to catch and a blow out of the flavour was quite common. Soon the actual birdfoods themselves became less effective as carp began to avoid the excessive flavour levels used by the majority of carp anglers.

A more enlightened attitude prevails these days. Most proprietary base mixes available from the bait companies now include not only a blend of birdfoods, but also selected proteins, effective binders, products such as dried kelp and kelp powder and a vitamin and mineral supplement so as to give the base mix a more attractive nutritional profile. This more balanced food source can be made even more attractive by using flavours and other additives at much lower levels. This has the effect of turning a birdfood mix from what was generally regarded as an attractor bait into a bait with a viable long term value; a food bait, in other words.

Like fishmeals, birdfood baits are usually almost instant with no need for extensive pre-baiting campaigns. Provided the flavour and attractor levels have been sensibly applied there is no reason why a well made birdfood bait will not last several seasons. I have used most of the more popular birdfoods and I have to say, I am always amazed at just how much of this type of bait carp are capable of eating. I know when my friends Steve Westbury and Nige Britton started fishing a 30-acre reservoir in North Devon they too found that the more they introduced, the better their results. Witness too the success of Bill Cottam and Brian Garner on the Shropshire water, The Mangrove Swamp. Using Evervite, a birdfood base mix from the Nutrabaits company, the pair baited the lake several times a week with five or six kilos of bait. The attractor level was an essential oil which was kept deliberately at a very low level so as to give the bait a season-long working life. Their results were staggering; better than any previous baiting campaign that had been mounted on the heavily fished water.

I can mirror their findings as I too have used considerable quantities of bird-food boilies in order to get the fish really feeding hard. At times it is even possible to make your bait the only one the carp will accept, so avidly do they react to a correctly applied and flavoured birdfood. Steve and Nige actually almost came to blows with one guy on the lake who became incensed with their heavy baiting level. He said there was no way the carp in the lake could possibly eat all that bait, they were poisoning the lake with rotting boilies, they were harming the fish and

Ken takes a dip with a fantastic linear mirror.

ruining the fishing for other anglers on the lake. At one point this guy actually stormed off the lake in a furious temper! You will not find it hard to accept that the guy has now channelled his energy into other less stressful pastimes. Needless to say, he was totally wrong. Nige and Steve caught all the known big fish in the lake over a three month period and every one of their captures was stuffed full of their bait.

I guess that nowadays, with a large number of bait companies all striving for their slice of the market, birdfoods must be one of the most cost-effective of their products. There must be a hundred and one different birdfood base mixes around these days, all claiming to empty lakes and put you and you alone out in front. But as we have already seen there are only so many birdfoods around and just about every mix will contain a percentage of one or more of the same ingredients.

J.E. Haith of Cleethorpes (I promised you that we'd hear more of this name) is one of the UK's largest supplier of specialist bird feeds. Some of their products are legendary and two in particular, Robin Red and Nectablend, must form the basis for just about every 'red' or 'yellow' mix going...unless the trade insists otherwise! Other well known birdfood mixes include The Birdfood Blend from Kevin Maddocks Baits, Big Seed Mix and Enervite Gold from Nutrabaits, and Red Seed, Yellow Seed and Spiced Seed Mixes from Solar Tackle; and there are a host of others. I would also guess that seed and birdfoods from J.E.Haith are probably the most widely used ingredients by those carp anglers who prefer to mix up their own unique recipes, rather than be confined to the dictates of the bait companies.

While J.E.Haith is not the only suppliers of bulk birdfood ingredients, it is probaly the best. The company certainly has the greatest range of products that can be applied to carp baits, and other well known brand names from the Haith stable include, PTX, Prosecto, Red Factor, Red Band, and of course, the famous Robin Red. The Sluis range of products is also very useful for making bait and Sluis CLO is probably one of the most widely used binders of carp mixes, while other products such as Sluis Mynar Bird food and Sluis Universal are also highly regarded.

Most birdfoods are based upon crushed seeds, ground hemp and ground pulses, biscuit meal and a wide selection of brans and other goodies. There are sweet mixes (PTX which has added molasses and honey) and savoury mixes (Prosecto which actually includes crushed insects in it!), and there are mixes that have little or no smell or taste but which are highly effective carp attractors (Nectablend, either ground or as it comes),

As their name implies, birdfoods are designed to improve and maintain the condition of show birds such as parakeets, canaries and budgies, and there are also some high energy products that are designed for racing pigeons, and there we have the key to the success of most birdfoods; high energy. Most birdfoods are usually blended at the manufacturers with an easily converted source of fat, often a food oil of some kind and it is the fat aspect of most birdfoods that makes them so useful as carp bait additives.

A decade or so back, before the fishmeal blitz hit the market, there were really only two types of nutritional baits; milk, egg and soya high protein baits and birdfood mixes. Both caught fish and both were often the subject of lengthy debate as to which was the better. The protein brigade insisted that carp need only a limited amount of fat and a high proportion of dietary protein in their food while devotees of less protein-biased baits advocated the less sophisticated, though equally effective low protein/high fat approach based on birdfoods and bulk ingredients. In retrospect it has since become abundantly clear that both schools of thought were more or less right in their beliefs. It was just that they both needed a little refining along the way so as to arrive at an ideal blend of the two. Nowadays many bait firms combine birdfoods and milk proteins in their base mixes to give the best of both worlds and it has become slightly less fashionable to talk of birdfood mixes simply as high fat or high energy baits. Yes, there is a high fat content, but by balancing this with a good supply of dietary protein in the base mix, birdfoods have now come of age as food baits in their own right. These days, while a reasonably high fat content is common in birdfood mixes, it is not the only significant factor in their success.

Birdfood baits are probably the second most popular type of bait used today (after fishmeals). They are particularly popular with anglers who make their own baits as they are very effective ingredients. Highly attractive, readily digestible, cheap to purchase in bulk and if used with high quality milk or egg proteins can make a very good long term bait.

The coarse nature of most birdfoods allows an almost immediate water exchange once the bait is in the lake: water goes in, flavour and attraction comes out. It has become popular to call birdfood baits high leakage baits, and you could be forgiven for thinking that this term refers to some totally new, ring-a-ding bait; it doesn't! A birdfood by any other name would smell as sweet!

Nevertheless, birdfood baits are currently enjoying a strong revival under this new guise of high leakage baits and as such they are proving very effective both as attractor baits (see earlier pieces on attraction and attractor baits) and as food baits, depending on the flavour levels used and the application of the bait from water to water. The swift leak-off of flavour from within the bait makes most birdfood baits

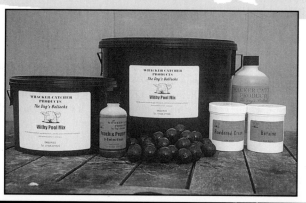

fairly instant in their attraction, yet it is clear that birdfood baits with a reasonably low flavour level are often quickly accepted as food by the carp and heavy baiting can reap significant rewards.

Many birdfoods contain their own in-built source of attraction. For instance, the famous and blindingly effective Robin Red Concentrate (from J.E. Haith) is a superb birdfood ingredient, but it is also a brilliant attractor in its own right, never mind simply as a nutritional food ingredient. Its unique smell and taste have tempted literally thousands of carp over the years and the dear old red stuff shows no sign of falling off just yet awhile. The active ingredients in Robin Red include the synthetic vitamin carophyll red, a blend of peppers and a selection of highly attractive spices. One of the best proprietary mixes of all time is the superb, Enervite from Nutrabaits, which relies to a certain degree, on Robin Red to attract carp. The success of this base mix has been astonishing, and you only need to look at the success of other carp bait mixes based on Robin Red to see just how great its pulling power can be.

A very simple yet effective bait can be made by mixing a birdfood with a bulk ingredient/binder such as semolina. Admittedly such a bait is unlikely to have a very long term future as a food bait in the accepted sense of the word, but a highly effective attractor bait can be made as follows:

250g Red factor (from J.E.Haith)
250g semolina
4ml Pineapple Nutrafruit
4ml Banana Nutrafruit
4ml KM Cream RM 30
2ml Sweet Cajouser.
20ml Multimino-PPC

This bait will catch carp, but it is likely to 'blow' in time due to the limited nutritional qualities and relatively high flavour levels. A better bait could be made by blending several birdfoods, together with a high quality binder, to form a more balanced food bait. Added milk protein would enhance the bait's drawing power still further. If it was then used with lower flavour levels a food bait would then be created. Such a bait might be:

150g Nectarblend
75g Prosecto
75g PTX
75g Robin Red
75g Calcium caseinate
50g Egg Albumin
4ml Sweet Nutraspice
8-10 drops Geranium Essential oil. (Nutrabaits)
20ml Multimino-PPC

As you can see, this bait is much better balanced than the previous example and the flavour levels are such that it should have a much longer catching life. This shows that simply taking one particular birdfood ingredient then adding lots of flavour and a bulk ingredient such as semolina is likely to create only a short term bait.

Other bait additives that complement most birdfood mixes include liver extracts, seafood extracts, Marmite or Bovril, liquid molasses or molasses meal and small amounts of milk and egg proteins to give the bait a more nutritional balance. As is now the case with the some fishmeal base mixes, combination baits may be the answer on your lake. Something like Big Seed Mix, with its added casein, kelp powder and milk based binders, may achieve better long term results than more simple combinations. However, for the most part, fairly simple mixes combining four or five different birdfoods along with a good quality binder such as Nutragel will have a very long catching life, provided you don't overload the flavours and other attractors. Just look at Julian Cundiff's results using Enervite Gold to see what I mean.

Like Julian, I too put great faith in well structured birdfood base mixes. The KM Birdfood Blend is an excellently balanced mix at a very affordable price, while Enervite Gold from Nutrabaits is as good as birdfoods get. I know that Julian had considerable success on the Gold using just one or two flavour combinations. His results speak for themselves, but you should bear in mind that he did not change the base mix in any way for over five years! That is proof if ever any were needed that a long term food bait strategy can be mounted using a good birdfood bait.

I too have used Enervite Gold to good effect. My own favourite recipe is:

500g Enervite Gold
4ml Cranberry Nutrafruit
2ml Cream Cajouser
2g Creamy Super Sweet
6 drops Bergamot Essential oil
20ml Corn Steep Liquor
2g Betaine HCI

That bait will catch anywhere, anytime, and if the flavour levels are not exceeded, it will lead to many successful seasons on any water.

10. High Protein HNV Baits

The issue of the effectiveness or otherwise of high protein, high nutritional value baits is something of a grey area these days. You either believe in them or you don't. There are no half measures. The carp world is divided as to their catching power. On one side you have the respected bait gurus such as Tim Paisley and Keith Sykes, on the other there are the advocates of less refined baits, the Lee Jacksons and Martin Lockes of this world.

Baits with a high protein content are nothing new. They have been around for many years, constantly adapted and refined as the years go by. Many believe that they are at the cutting edge of bait technology, the way forward into areas of bait research that have previously only been touched upon. It is quite possible that, despite all the experiments and developments on this type of bait, so far we have only scratched the surface of what can be a highly complex issue.

I think that the best way I can explain the thinking behind high protein baits is to spend some time looking at my personal experiences, so I hope readers will indulge me here.

First of all, I should nail my colours to the mast and state that I am a huge fan of HNVs and have been since the beginning of 1985. When I first started using them, bait technology in general was light years away from what it is today and protein HNVs were the most advanced and certainly the most efficient way of catching carp. Nowadays the science of bait technology has become almost an art form and it is now quite possible to formulate highly attractive and nutritious baits that are probably better than the original protein baits I was using over a decade ago.

Fishmeal baits with a high nutritional value are probably at the pinnacle of modern baits and are in all probability as near a perfect carp bait as we can get at the present time. However, even they have their drawbacks, particularly during the winter months when it is quite likely that they are less effective.

In the mid to late 80s high protein baits turned me from a guy who caught his share of carp into one that caught far more than his share! For much of this time I fished College Reservoir in Cornwall where Carole and I did exceptionally well, so I hope you won't mind if this chapter is somewhat anecdotal in its approach. I will leave you to make up your own mind after you have read of my experiences and maybe compared them to a situation that you may have experienced where my results may point the way for you. Anyway, as there have been more words written about high protein baits with an exceptionally high nutritional value, a few more won't hurt!

As I have already explained, a bait with a high nutritional value can be defined as any bait that provides a complete balanced food that benefits carp nutritionally. OK?

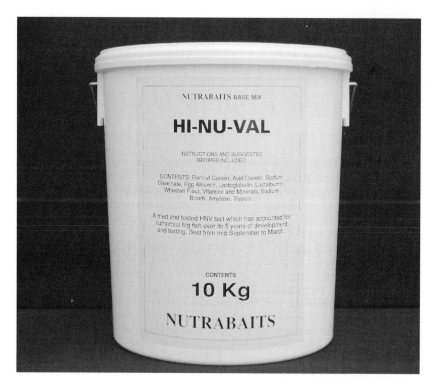

Hi-Nu-Val – just look at the list of ingredients.

No, not OK. That is too wide a definition if we are restricting ourselves to talking about high protein baits. You see, any well formulated fishmeal or birdfood bait can be a nutritional HNV. Provided the bait is capable of being used to the carp's benefit then it is perfectly acceptable to talk about say, Big Fish Mix or The Four Seasons Mix as HNVs. But for old fogies like Tim Paisley and I – he's even older than I am! – any reference to an HNV bait will automatically mean one with a milk, egg and possibly, a soya protein base and with a very high overall protein content. In addition there will be a well structured vitamin and mineral content and just enough fat to provide a convertible energy source. And I'm NOT talking about 20-30ml of fish oils here. More likely the fat source will be 5ml olive oil or sesame seed oil.

When you introduce a high protein HNV to the water, your intention is to provide a bait that is a food source. One that, when introduced in sufficient quantity, is enough to get carp feeding on that bait in numbers, coming to regard it as an essential part of their day to day diet. Now you might say, I can achieve that using particles or fishmeals or just about any other nutritional food source. True, but many believe that the best possible results can only be achieved by using a high protein base.

The Wilton Principle, though not as protein-biased as subsequent ideas, lays down the basic nutritional concept and advocates of protein HNVs have simply taken Fred's theory one step further. In the early- to mid-80s I was lucky to be taken under the Tim Paisley wing. The top quality bait Tim and friends had put together was milk and egg protein-based. A low level message (in my case 1 drop of Garlic Oil and 2ml of Blue Cheese flavour – enough simply to provide a recognition signal), was added and a baiting programme commenced.

Our baiting campaign began at Christmas 1984 though we didn't start fishing the lake until February 1985. The first carp to come out on the bait was a 29lb 5oz mirror. Next trip was in early March and it kicked off with a 20lb 8oz mirror. The third fish out weighed 31lb 3oz and was the biggest known fish in the lake. Fourth and fifth fish were both mid twenties and the sixth fish was a repeat capture of the thirty at 31lb 5oz, a record for the water that stands to this day. Some may say that this run of very big fish was simply a coincidence, that the bait had nothing to do with it, or that it was simply the attractors that were responsible for the result. Rubbish! Tim had given the recipe to a very few selected anglers to field test on various venues and though I didn't know it at the time, our results were being mirrored on selected waters all around the UK: some coincidence!

Following those initial captures, the bait went from strength to strength. As 1985 came and went our confidence in it grew to such an extent that we simply knew we would catch wherever we fished on the lake. That confidence became a rock-solid foundation for what followed: we went on to use the bait more or less unchanged for the next five years with astonishing results; well over 1200 carp between the two of us from College alone! Not surprisingly those results made a protein HNV fundamentalist of me!

The recipe has been published before but I'll repeat it now for to my mind it is a bait that will hold its own on any water:

200g Express Food Industry's Rennet Casein.

75g New Zealand Lactalbumin

75g egg albumin

50g Bengers (a food drink containing the protein specific enzyme Tripsin)

50g Davina Body Build (also enzyme-based, a weight lifter's supplement containing another enzyme specific to milk protein, Bromelain).

50g Vitmin (a vitamin and mineral supplement supplied by the bait company S.B.S.)

2ml Richworth Blue Cheese

2g Cajoler (now from Nutrabaits)

1 drop Garlic Essential Oil

2 Quest Enzyme Digest tablets

25ml Minamino.

Add eggs, roll out to 20mm baits and boil 12-15 at a time for NO MORE THAN 50 seconds. (In winter we cut this down to 35 seconds). It is vital not to add too many baits to the boiling water. The pan must not come off the boil for one second. The boiling time is also vital. Exceeding the ceiling of 50 seconds can denature the proteins within the bait, thus destroying all that you have striven so hard to achieve. The egg albumin is included in the recipe to help decrease the boiling time. Though it is expensive, it is a vital part of the bait. Leave it out and you will find you need to boil the baits for twice as long, thus spoiling the bait.

In 1987 I cut by half the rennet casein content, adding acid casein instead. At the same time I substituted a pungent smelling additive, N-Butyric acid, for the cheese flavour and added 15ml Davina Liquid Liver to the mix. Finally the bait reached its zenith in 1988 when I managed to get hold of a reliable crystalline source of Betaine HCl. With the bait at its highest stage of development its pulling power was truly awesome. I recall one trip in October '87 when I had twenty carp including eight twenties in a 60-hour session.

No matter how many small but subtle changes I made to the bait, the base ingredients stayed the same...and it kept on working!

The recipe above is a classic HNV that did exactly what it was supposed to do: provide long term preoccupation on a good food bait. I won't say the carp in College HAD to have my bait, but there were times when I'm sure they were queueing up for it!

All the baits were frozen and used straight from the freezer, being transported to the water in large capacity Thermos flasks. When you are using a high proportion of milk proteins in your bait, it is important to ensure that they are as fresh as possible. Think about it. Doesn't milk quickly go off if you leave it out of the 'fridge? This principle was so ingrained in me that I would rather throw unused baits into the rubbish bin than introduce them to the water.

To what extent the enzymes in the base mix played their part is hard to say. There were occasions when the bait was noticeably much more attractive, but that could have been down to any number of factors. To be honest, the kitchen at home is not the right place to carry out scientific measurements and experiments with highly complex chemicals such as protein-splitting enzymes!

All I know is that I would far rather have them inside my bait than not at all, whether they worked as intended every time or not. And I have to admit with hindsight that I doubt if one mix in thirty allowed the enzymes to do their work as they were supposed to. But when they did...oh brother. Did they EVER work!

We went down some decidedly dodgy tracks looking for the ultimate bait during the eighties! I can remember using a protein digesting enzyme that started eating my skin (which is, after all, protein itself). Another was so active it was practically impossible to achieve a solid ball of paste; the enzyme just kept on breaking down the proteins in the paste resulting in a sticky mess that was impossible to work with.

However, from time to time on those rare occasions when I am positive that I managed to achieve the reaction I intended, the results we had were outstanding. On these occasions a boilie would break down to a mush in the water within a maximum of twelve hours. Obviously some sort of reaction was taking place once the baits hit the water. I only realised this after I brought in a succession of empty hairs, something that happened too often for it to have been a coincidence. From then on I recast every three hours (if I hadn't had a take – a rare event). Dear me! Did those 'special' mixes ever catch. I just wish it wasn't all so hit and miss in my unscientific hands.

It has to be said that milk and egg protein bases are decidedly out of fashion these days. This may well be due to the high cost of such base mixes. Sure, they are expensive, no question, and if you can achieve the same result at half the cost, why not? But the fact remains, some of the best anglers in the country still use protein HNVs. The food messages from a properly put together protein HNV are practically irresistible to carp, and you don't necessarily need to rely on a flavour to draw attention to the bait. If you get it right, the breakdown activity of the bait is sufficient to attract carp.

The correct application of a protein HNV bait is vital if you are to achieve the result it deserves. You are aiming for LONG TERM preoccupation, not a quick fix. If you can get the carp in your water to go out of their way to look for your bait, that is the way you get under their guard, by instilling confidence in the bait. In 1985 we baited up at College on a regular basis for a full year, fifty-two weeks a year. We used a quarter of a ton of base mix alone in the first 12 months! From then on it was like shelling peas!

Remember, we were fishing for about three hundred fish in about 40 acres and the intention was to get every fish in the lake accustomed to the bait. I think we achieved this and the results speak for themselves. Usually we took twelve mixes for a weekend session and often used them all particularly if we were on the wind and the fish were obviously having it.

The attractor level you use in any HNV bait is vital, but it is particularly so in protein HNVs. Remember, the attractor is there to provide a label with which the carp associates food. After a while it will come to recognise that smell and will react positively to it. You are not trying to make the carp eat the bait simply by the smell of the attractor. The attractor is there to enable the carp to locate the bait time and time again.

I have already mentioned that amino acids hold the key to successful attraction but it is important to understand that these are extremely sensitive to heat. Keep the boiling time to a minimum with ANY HNV but particularly with protein HNVs containing amino acids, either in crystalline form or in liquid.

I'd be the last to tell you that high protein HNVs are the be all and end all of carp baits. These days it is easy enough to buy a reputable proprietary base mix and achieve almost the same result, but if you are prepared to spend the money, take the risks and get it right, I still firmly believe that there is no better carp bait.

CARP 'R' US

THE RIG SPECIALISTS

P.O. BOX 4200, SUDBURY, SUFFOLK CO10 7LE
Tel: (24hrs) 01787 282370 Fax: 01787 282380

A GOOD BAIT DESERVES A GOOD RIG - HERE ARE 4 THAT WONT LET YOU DOWN

THE NEW LONGSHANK 'NAILER' IS A VERY VERSATILE AND DEADLY HOOK, USED EXTENSIVELY BY KEVIN MADDOCKS

MK.2 WITHY POOL RIG
(BUOYANT BAITS)

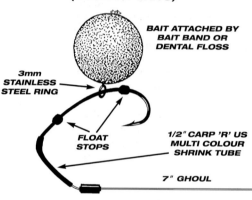

BAIT ATTACHED BY BAIT BAND OR DENTAL FLOSS

3mm STAINLESS STEEL RING

FLOAT STOPS

1/2" CARP 'R' US MULTI COLOUR SHRINK TUBE

7" GHOUL

SOLAR DEPTH CHARGE WEIGHT OR SPLIT SHOT

THIS RIG MUST BE OVERSHOTTED

SPINNER RIG
(POP-UP RIG ONLY)

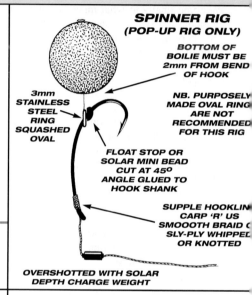

BOTTOM OF BOILIE MUST BE 2mm FROM BEND OF HOOK

3mm STAINLESS STEEL RING SQUASHED OVAL

NB. PURPOSELY MADE OVAL RING ARE NOT RECOMMENDED FOR THIS RIG

FLOAT STOP OR SOLAR MINI BEAD CUT AT 45° ANGLE GLUED TO HOOK SHANK

SUPPLE HOOKLINK CARP 'R' US SMOOOTH BRAID OR SLY-PLY WHIPPED OR KNOTTED

OVERSHOTTED WITH SOLAR DEPTH CHARGE WEIGHT

WITHY POOL BOTTOM RIG WITH REVERSE HAIR

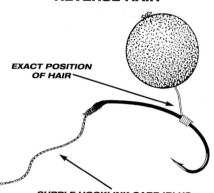

EXACT POSITION OF HAIR

SUPPLE HOOKLINK CARP 'R' US SMOOOTH OR SLY-PLY

EFFECT OF RIG IS TO ACT IN THE NORMAL WAY UNTIL EJECTED. THE FORCE OF THE BAIT BEING BLOWN OUT CAUSES THE HOOK TO TURN IN THE MOUTH, SNAGGING THE SKIN INSTANTLY.

BLOW BACK RIG
POP-UP OR BOTTOM RIG

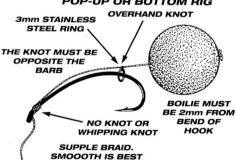

OVERHAND KNOT

3mm STAINLESS STEEL RING

THE KNOT MUST BE OPPOSITE THE BARB

BOILIE MUST BE 2mm FROM BEND OF HOOK

NO KNOT OR WHIPPING KNOT

SUPPLE BRAID. SMOOTH IS BEST

HOW TO MAKE:
1. TIE LOOP IN END OF BRAID FOR HAIR.
2. TIE ON STAINLESS STEEL RING USING SINGLE OVERHAND KNOT.
3. SLIDE RING OVER HOOK POINT TO A POSITION WHERE THE KNOT ON THE RING IS OPPOSITE THE BARB.
4. DEPENDING ON SIZE OF BOILIE BEING USED ADJUST THE DISTANCE OF THE LENGTH OF HAIR BY HOLDING RING AND PULLING THE BRAID.

11. 50/50 Mixes

We come finally to what many would regard as the bottom end of the market as far as base mixes are concerned, the so-called 50/50 mixes. I am not sure how or why these baits acquired their name but I believe it was originally the Richworth company that coined the term to refer to a mix that was supposed to be fifty percent protein and fifty percent carbohydrate. To be honest I am not sure where they got the fifty percent protein values from as the base mix was mainly semolina and soya flour, but still...

Nowadays the term 50/50 mix is generally taken to mean any base mix with a low food value that is kind on the wallet, easy to roll and can be adapted for use either as an attractor bait or as a reasonable, if short-term, food bait.

The main ingredients used in these types of bait are semolina, soya flour, maize meal and maize flour, and various bait companies tweak up their own proprietary base mixes with little individual touches of their own. For instance, I am assured that Nutrabaits adds, "A little personal touch from the boys up North," whatever the hell that means. Personally I think that Andy James passes his hands over every bag and whispers some magic incantation or other!

A fairly typical 50/50 recipe would comprise the following:

250g Yellow semolina.
250g Soya Flour
100g Brown sugar or icing sugar.
15-25ml of Strawberry Nutrafruit
1-2ml Geranium Oil
5-10ml Liquid Hermesetas (as a sweetener).

You may think that there is too much flavour in there and with some justification, but the reason for the high level is that you need to boil the baits for around five minutes and a great deal of the flavour is lost during the boiling process. That said, those flavour levels are on the high side even allowing for some evaporation.

But as we have already seen low food value baits such as 50/50 mixes are ideal as attractor baits and there is no need for any significant food value. Attractor baits catch mainly on the strength of the flavours and other attractors and the high inclusion levels shown above are part and parcel of such an approach.

The recipe catches carp because while it is of relatively low food value it imposes little or no strain on the carp's digestive system, as it passes through the digestive tract in less than half an hour or so. The fish derive little nutritional input from the bait, so they need to eat a great deal of it in order to obtain even the smallest dietary fulfilment from it. It follows then that for the best results on this kind of bait you need to put a lot in to satisfy the carp.

This is where the basic flaw in high flavour/low food value baits arises. Mass baiting will certainly catch fish, but not forever, unlike a similarly applied Food

Bait such as a high protein mix like Hi-Nu-Val, a well formulated fishmeal mix such as Big Fish Mix, or a birdfood bait such as Enervite Gold or the Big Seed Mix. Properly flavoured with a delicate blend of attractors these types of bait will last almost indefinitely.

The bait shown above will lose its effectiveness comparatively quickly for either (or maybe both) of the following two reasons: 1) Because eventually the carp realise that they are having to expend an awful lot of energy picking up a great many baits without even maintaining their dietary status quo, or: 2) Because they become wary or even repelled by a high flavour level which they may come to associate with the above or with danger (see also the chapter on attractor baits). Either way, poorly thought out, low food value baits are only a short term answer to the problem of how to catch carp.

In terms of digestibility – or rather, the rate at which these base mixes are processed by a carp – it is hard to beat simple soya/semolina base mixes, but if you also want to include an element of nutritional quality to the base mix, without at the same time increasing the expense, you can now go for a low food base that has added digestible whey proteins such as The Nutramix from Nutrabaits, or the 50/50 Boilie Mix from the KM Range.

Maize meal is another product with a high food content that can be substituted for part or all of either the semolina or the soya flour content of the recipe shown above. Maize meal has a protein value of around 55%, but not all of this can be used by the carp as vegetable proteins are generally thought to be less digestible. However, a more nutritional bait that can be used over a reasonably long period would be:

150g yellow semolina.
150g full fat soya flour
150g maize meal
25g vitamin and mineral supplement.
25g liver powder.
3ml Cranberry Nutrafruit
2ml Sweet Cajouser.
25ml Minamino

Add eggs, roll out into paste balls then boil for 2 minutes.

That recipe can be used throughout a summer campaign but come the autumn and winter months and you may find its effectiveness might drop off dramatically as the fish tend to feed on baits with a better nutritional worth.

Having stated my own personal preference for the more sophisticated types of base mixes, you may find it surprising to read that I often use cheaper baits as well. There are angling and baiting situations that simply cry out for these mixes and I have no hesitation in suggesting a few to you.

First of all if you are fishing on a budget and have to watch the pennies, 50/50 mixes offer the lowest cost per pound of any of the carp bait base mixes. Provided you are prepared to ring the changes on flavours as soon as you feel your results may be dropping off (and this may happen a lot more quickly than you could possibly imagine), 50/50 mixes will catch you lots of carp.

Secondly, for fishing abroad there is little to beat a 50/50 mix. Add a preservative of some kind such as Preservabait from Nutrabaits and then dry the baits thoroughly and you have a bait that will catch big French carp for the duration of your holiday. Indeed, many top French anglers use nothing else for their summer long campaigns. The drying is a significant factor in baits treated with Preservabait and I have found that by far the best way to dry them is on the purpose-designed drying racks made by Gardner Tackle. These are simply the best in the business, but if you can't afford a set then the next best method is to store the finished baits in an old pair of tights, or an onion sack. Hang this in the airing cupboard for a week or so and you will have baits that will harden and dry out and last a very long time.

You can make very good attractor baits from 50/50 mixes, either for hook-baits only or even for a baiting campaign. Personally I only use over-flavoured hookbaits when I am fishing in France. (See chapter on Hookbaits.)

Finally I like to use low food value ingredients when making either Boilie Soup or a loose groundbait. By adding water and flavour to a kilo of 50/50 mix and a kilo of yellow semolina you achieve a very good groundbait that can be mixed up wet and formed into balls or baited into the margins via a Cobra Groundbaiter.

There is no doubting the effectiveness of 50/50 baits and provided that you don't try to elevate their status by regarding them as food baits, you will certainly catch carp. By realising their limitations as a carp FOOD, rather than as a carp BAIT, you can use low food value baits to catch carp from all manner of waters. But you must be alert at all times for the slightest indication that your results are not quite what they were when the bait first started going in. Provided you are on the ball and ready to change either base mix or flavour (or both) at the first sign that the fish may be getting tired of them, you will benefit from the use of 50/50 mixes.

The main difference between a low food bait and a bait with a good nutri-tional balance is that when things get slow on the latter, all it may take to get them feeding hard once again is a really heavy bait up. Put ten or a dozen mixes in all around the lake and if the bait is based on a mix with a good food value and the flavour and attractor level is a long term one, you should easily be able to re-estab-lish the bait. On the other hand, if things get slow on a low food value bait, the LAST thing you want to do is pile yet more of it in. If they seem reluctant to eat one or two mixes, they will certainly not eat ten or a dozen of the same mix.

50/50 are a perfectly acceptable alternative bait and given their limitations can be used with confidence on any type of water, be it a hard fished venue or a lake that's never been fished before.

PARTRIDGE
OF REDDITCH

Carp & Specimen Hunter hooks from Partridge. Round eyes, sharp needle points & neat barbs or with barbless patterns with strong high carbon steel wire, all together make these the finest quality hooks available.

Partridge hooks, available in our traditional black finish, grey shadow, or our newly developed Black Nickel finish.

They are the choice of world renown and respected fishermen such as Kevin Maddocks, who understand the need for consistent quality & unsurpassed performance.

Choose from our extensive range of quality hooks. Each made in Redditch, England to exacting standards and with an unconditional guarantee.

> Good bait deserve good hooks.
>
> Old carp proverb.

A selection from our extentive range.

Z15XLBN Kevin Maddocks Boilie Carp Extra Long
Sizes: 2,4,6,8 & 10
New **Design**
New **Black Nickel coating**

Z14BN Special "Piggyback" Bent hook
Sizes: 2,4, 6 & 8
New **Design**
New **Black Nickel coating**

Z11 Kevin Maddocks Hair Rig Hooks
Sizes: 1,2,4,6,8 & 10

Z1Y Jack Hilton Carp Barbless
Sizes: 1,2,4,6,8 & 10

Z18 WS Barbless Arrowpoint Specimen Hunter Hooks
Sizes: 2,4,6 & 8

Z6 Sidley Baitholder
Sizes: 1, 2 & 4

Z3 Semi-Barbless Pike Trebles
Sizes: 4, 6, 8 & 10

Ask your dealer for more information or contact us at the address below.

PARTRIDGE OF REDDITCH LIMITED
MOUNT PLEASANT REDDITCH WORCESTERSHIRE ENGLAND B97 4JE
TELEPHONE: +44 (0) 1527 543 555 FAX: +44 (0) 1527 546 956
email: hooks@partridge-of-redditch.com

12. Home-Made Base Mixes

There are some mixes that claim to be totally different to the everyday, run-of-the-mill, standard mixes, but in reality 99.9% are based on one of these four types of mix we have already looked at in the preceeding chapters. So what about the other 0.1%?

Despite what the bait companies themselves might tell you, there is very little that is 'different' in their so-called alternative base mixes. Sure, there may be some subtle addition that makes the mix stand out, but by and large the magic ingredient will be some form of fishmeal, birdfood etc, etc.

That said, base mixes such as The Grange Mix from Mainline, The Quench Mixes from Solar, Nash Bait's S Mix and the Total Hemp Mix and The Biolix, both from Nutrabaits are unique enough in their make up to deserve to be entered in the 'different' bait category. These apart most base mixes, be they cheap and cheerful or very expensive they are likely to fall into one of our four main categories.

A recent addition to the market is the Total Hemp Mix from Nutrabaits. This product can truly claim to be 'different' for it contains over 75% pure hemp to which are added binders and proteins. My recent experiments with the base mix, albeit in the winter months with correspondingly low water temperatures, have been very encouraging; who knows how much more effective the bait will be during the summer when warm water temperatures will more effectively be able to get to work on the bait's inherent oil content. As we all know, hemp is full of oil and I can really see the mix coming into its own as a summer mix. It truly can be called an alternative bait; it is totally different to any base mix that has gone before, but given its expected success, no doubt there will be hemp based mixes flooding the market in the not-to-distant future!

From the previous chapters on base mixes you can be forgiven for thinking that base mixes from the bait companies are the ONLY type of mix. That simply is not the case and if you are limited to a low cost budget there are many ways you can cut your costs without lowering your standards, by making your own baits out of base mixes that you have formulated yourself. This chapter acts only as a basic guide to home made mixes, the rest I leave to your imagination.

Prior to the recent carp fishing explosion we all used to muck along quite nicely, each thinking that only we had the magic "Ingredient X" which would change our lives...I wish! I can recall when I started fishing College Reservoir near Penryn in Cornwall. At the time there were only two carp men fishing the lake, and both were using relatively poor, old fashioned baits. Carole and I had been using a bait on other South West carp lakes to very good effect. It was a recipe that had been given to us by my oldest friend, Bill Speed when we fished together at Waveney Valley Lakes in the late 70s. It was also Bill who put me onto the hair

Two popular ingredients used in home-made base mixes.

rig, but that is another story, However, with Bill's bait AND the hair rig, Carole and I had a giant head start over every other carp man in the county.

The bait was as simple as you could wish, a mix comprised as follows:

250g ground Nectablend
50g Wheat Gluten
50g Robin Red Concentrate.

The flavour was either Hutchinson's original Scopex or Geoff Kemp's Maple at 10ml, no sweetener, no liquid foods. Nowt, in fact. As simple a bait as you could find, one that worked a treat in the late 70s and early 80s. The bait took fish from every water we chucked it into, including Cut Mill, Homersfield, Waveney Valley, Taplow, Longfield, Bury Hill, Wheal Rashleigh, Salamander Lake and, of course, College.

It was 1980: Nutrabaits was seven years away from formation and I was still five years away from acquiring the bait that would change my carp fishing life (see the chapter on High Protein HNVs), and Kevin Maddocks was just about to stun the carp world with the publication of Carp Fever. The bait section in that book, written jointly by Kevin and John Baker, represented a huge stride forward for many carp men. It pointed out that a lot more thought needed to go into creating a successful carp bait. Chucking ten ml of flavour into eggs then adding a random mix of dry ingredients was no longer going to be enough.

But for the kick-off of our long campaign on College it was enough, and it caught well. We came home after our first day trip and made another 5,000 baits. The following day we returned and caught a hatful, and the rest is history. Eventually we refined the original birdfood bait considerably. Advice from Bill, who was tuned into the Home Counties carp grapevine suggested lower flavour levels, a sweetener and some kind of liver-based attractor. By 1982 we were hitting Waveney with a bait that seemed a great deal more sophisticated. It was:

250g Nectablend – ground to a powder in a coffee grinder.
50g Egg Albumin
75g Casilan (calcium caseinate)
75g Robin Red Concentrate.
50g Equivite Vitamin Supplement (a health preparation for horses)
8ml Maple flavour
1ml Geranium essential oil
5ml liquid Hermesetas
15ml Liquid liver
5-6 size 2 eggs.
Boil for 90 seconds, sieve and turn out onto a dry towel, then allow to dry.

That recipe was stunning. The lower flavour level allowed the higher level of Robin Red to shine through. The smell and taste of Robin Red is unique and it has an incredible pulling power. In addition we had added liquid liver, and a milk and an egg protein, which allowed us to reduce the boiling time. The bait now had a much more pronounced nutritional signal and could be viewed as a food bait rather than an attractor bait, as was the case with Bill's original recipe. Though the above recipe is probably seen as old fashioned these days, it is one of the most effective recipes I ever put together. I'm sure it would catch well from most waters, even today.

The brand-named ingredients in the two recipes shown come from our old friend J.E.Haith & Son of Cleethorpes. Where would be be without them! The company sells enough birdfood ingredients to keep you busy for years. As for the proteins, you can buy egg albumin from specialist cake and ice cream shops, while the Casilan is sold in some larger chemists shops.

I will not pretend that egg albumin and Casilan are cheap and if your pocket is not as deep as you would like it to be, you can cut out these two along with 2 ounces of Nectarblend and substitue these for 6-8oz of yellow semolina. Obviously you are detracting from the nutritional aspect of the bait and it will probably not have such a prolonged catching life, but that is one of the paradoxes of carp fishing: the better the bait, the more you have to pay for it, but the longer it will last.

Here's another recipe that you can make up from readily available ingredients. Again it features semolina as an equal part of the mix. The other fifty percent is Haith's Red Factor. As a base mix it is cheap and cheerful, but it catches carp. The recipe is as follows:

225g yellow semolina
225g Red factor.
50g Icing sugar
Flavours and attractors of your choice. Why not try:
3ml Strawberry Nutrafruit
3ml Cream Cajouser
6 drops bergamot oil.

That flavour combination is tried and tested and should work on the above simple recipe.

Chemists shops, delicatessens and health food stores are a constant source of inspiration for the carp man who wants to make baits on a budget. Baby foods, liquid foods, pure proteins (Sanatogen, Casilan, etc), health drinks, body building supplements, they are all useful products that can be used in carp baits.

Full fat soya flour and maize meal can be blended together with yellow semolina to make a reasonable base; add dear old ubiquitous Robin Red to the mix and you're away. Simply mix 125g of each of the four ingredients, then flavour the mix with 25-30ml Minanino (from the chemists) and 5ml of Nutrabaits Sweet Nutraspice. Roll the paste into balls and boil for two to three minutes. Simple but effective.

You can make a cheap and cheerful fishmeal mix if you like. Look out for farmer's supply shops and warehouses. You will probably notice some fishmeals that are intended solely for fertiliser but I urge you to ignore these. They are probably old meals and the oil content may well be rancid. They are rubbish for making carp baits. Look out instead for sacks of fishmeal-based pellets which will be marked as feeds for sheep and pigs. The pellets can be ground down to a powder and then used in a bait. Also keep an eye out for a processed white fishmeal called PROVIMI 66. This is an excellent ingredient with a high protein and oil content. It is used in many proprietary fishmeal mixes to form up to 50% of the base.

You will need a vitamin and mineral supplement of some kind to balance the food value of your bait. Turn now to the area of the warehouse set aside for equine products and buy tubs of dried seaweed, Equivite Vitamin Suuplement and a small tub of Codlivine. All of these can be used to form a simple base mix. This recipe will serve you well:

200g ground pellets (could be trout pellets if you like)
75g Codlivine
75g Equivite
50g Dried seaweed
100g Sluis CLO (from pet shops)

Blend the dry ingredients together by shaking them thoroughly in a heavy duty polythene bag. Then add the mixed powders to the eggs. Flavours are a matter for personal choice but if you are looking for a perfect blend, try Nutrabaits Caviar and Black Pepper essential oil. That combination has already accounted for at least three fifty pound (22.7kg) carp from the UK alone.

Yeast is a brilliant addition to any base mix. You can turn a bog standard, boring old birdfood bait into a real steamer by the simple addition of Phillip's yeast Mixture (PYM). Guess where you can get this stuff? That's right! J.E.Haith!

Here is a recipe that includes two sources of yeast:

200g ground Nectablend.
50g PYM
50g Brewer's Yeast (home brewing shops and chemists).
50g Robin Red
50g Liver Powder.
100g Sluis CLO (from pet shops)
15ml liquid liver
25ml Minamino
1 teaspoonful of salt.

Add eggs and boil for 90 seconds.

There are so many readily available foodstuffs around today that are absolutely crying out to be included in a carp bait of some kind. Just look along the shelves of the chemists shops to see what I mean. Or browse around farmers supply warehouses, pet shops, equestrian suppliers and Indian and Chinese delis.

Ken with a fabulous fish of 34$^1/_2$ pounds (15.7kg).

One thing you owe it to yourself to do is ring J.E. Haith and get them to send you their price list...and before you ask, no, I am not on commission for the company. Ask any of even the largest bait firms in the UK: they will tell you that not even THEY can get a discount, and they order their Haith ingredients by the tonne. John Haith himself is a notorious skin-flint and the idea that he would put a smelly old carp angler on commission would have him rolling about! Quite simply, the only reason I mention the company at all is that it is an absolute gold mine for the aspiring carp man who wants to make his own base mixes. If it wasn't for J.E.Haith and Son many of today's bait companies would never make a living!

13. Ready-made Boilies

It seems strange to have come this far in the book without getting more heavily involved with what are arguably the most widely used baits in carp fishing, ready-made boilies.

From the moment of their inception way back in the early eighties ready-made baits have accounted for literally thousands of big carp. Nowadays all the major bait companies have a range of these baits in their product list and some of the best come from the KM Professional Range. You only have to look at the success enjoyed by Kevin Maddocks – the brains behind the KM Bait business – to see just how fantastically effective they can be. Kevin's exploits on some of the hardest waters in Europe speak for themselves. Together with his fishing partner Alan Taylor he has caught massive carp from many of the popular 'circuit' waters in France, Germany, Holland and Belgium; lakes with names to dream about. Lac du Der-Chatecoq (witness the incredible video, Ton-Up at Lac du Der), Foret d'Orient (see the video, Quest for Big carp), Lac de St Cassien, Lac du Causse at Brieve-le-Gaillard, the Belgian canals and the Dutch inland seas, culminating in a fabulous personal best of 55lb from a lake in southern France. All this success was down to ready-mades from the KM Professional range of ready-mades. Need further proof?

The history of the development of ready-mades is well documented. Briefly...

...They were originally marketed by the Richworth company started by Clive Deidrich and his friend and partner, the late Malcolm Winkworth – hence the name! The first ready-mades were available only as frozen baits as the gas flush system originally envisaged to preserve the boilies proved ineffective. So too did vacuum packing. In a bid to get their bait launched in a satisfactory state of preservation Richworth rented out freezers to dozens of selected shops and they supplied the baits ready-frozen to be stocked in their freezers.

This was satisfactory but only up to a point. Steps were taken to try and find a suitable human grade food preservative so that the baits could be bagged and sold unfrozen with a long shelf life. Much of the initial work was carried out by laboratories specialising in research into preserving human foodstuffs, so by the time a finished process was perfected, the preservatives and other additives suggested by the labs were inevitably up to the highest human grade standards.

As soon as this type of bait first hit the shops it revolutionised carp baits completely. Kevin Maddocks Maestro and Duncan Kay's Purple Patch boilies were the very first popular shelf-life ready-mades. I well remember the very first time I used a Maestro shelf life boilie. At the time I was held completely spellbound by the mystique and allure of the 'heavy science' enzyme-based high protien HNV baits, a true bait fundamentalist, if you like. I can tell you, it took quite a leap of faith to put a ready-made on the hair. The fact that I was fishing in France made me a bit

The Kevin Maddocks range of ready-mades has a proven track record of success.

easier in my mind, but not a lot! I was actually astonished when I caught carp on that KM boilie. What a plonker! I should have known by the bait's history that it was a red hot catcher. Yet still I had to pinch myself to make sure I wasn't dreaming! Townley catching on ready-mades! Perish the thought.

A lot of water has flowed through my landing net mesh since then, often accompanied by a great many big carp, and ready-mades have accounted for a lot of these big lumps. I now use them both at home and abroad and if I think that I can get a better result using ready-mades, than I will on home made baits, I have no hesitation in using them. It is really a question of assessing the water, the carp you are fishing for and the amount of bait pressure they are under and if you think that a ready-made boilie is the bait for the job, use it!

By now I hope you will have read and understood enough of this book to be able to assess your own needs and you should be able to make the right decision as to what type of bait may be best suited for any particular angling situation that confronts you. I have outlined quite a few recipes and the thinking behind them so there is really no excuse for anyone these days to make up a poor home made bait. However, if you are one of those head-in-the sand anglers who still insists that it is perfectly OK to throw a bucket of flavour over a load of rubbishy old ingredients, all thrashed together in a mixing bowl, and calling it a bait, you are going to get hammered off the water by any of today's modern ready-made baits. Be under no illusions, ready-mades will catch far more fish than a badly made, home produced job, and under some carp angling conditions will even catch better than anything you can make at home, no matter how good the base mix, ingredients, flavours or attractors.

If that's the case, then why aren't they the only bait worth using, you may be saying to yourself? Well like many other aspects of carp fishing, life just ain't that easy!

For a start, you'll note I said, under SOME carp angling conditions, not under ALL of them. There may be situations when a ready-made simply won't do the job, others when a ready-made is THE bait to be on.

As an example of just how outstanding they can be, I'd like to quote the campaign of well respected carp man Bernie Loftus on the mega-hard, Harefield Lake. The water has seen it all and the carp are spooky and cautious as hell. Bernie went in with a massive baiting campaign using Richworth Tutti-Fruiti ready-mades. All the regulars scoffed and said the bait had blown long ago, but Bernie confounded them with a steady run of big fish that blew the socks off the other baits on the water.

It wasn't a long run of success and after five or six weeks the bait began to lose its effectiveness, but by that time Bernie had his hit. Who needed a longer catching life? The damage was done. Result: Bernie = Loads o' carp: others = naff all!

Of course, the campaign was not cheap,for ready-mades are expensive to produce and package. As modern ready-mades become more sophisticated, with better nutritional properties, more effective attractors and so on, the price has increased even further, but if you want top quality ready-mades such as those from the KM Professional range, you have to be prepared to pay the price.

The machinery required to make ready-mades is usually purpose-built, or adapted from equipment for confectionery manufacture. That kind of technology doesn't come cheap. Add to that the cost of the flavours, colours, eggs, sweeteners, preservatives and packaging and you will understand why they are usually more expensive than home made boilies.

On the other side of the coin there is the sheer drudgery of making baits at home. Sure, you can make them cheaper, and you have more control over the finished product, but what an armpit of a job it is! Personally I owe a debt of thanks to Richard Gardner of Gardner Tackle for designing all those wonderful gadgets that take the worst of the boredom out of bait making at home...but it is still the job I hate most in carp fishing!

It is perhaps a bit hard for newcomers to the sport to sort out the distinction between ready-mades and home produced baits. To try and make understanding the application of both types of bait a bit easier, can I just explain the how, when and why I use ready-mades.

First off, if I am using a groundbait of some kind I usually put a few ready-mades in as well. Boilies fished over the top of particles or seed baits has always been a successful method and once the required level of preoccupation on the groundbait is achieved it makes little difference what is on the hair. It needs to be smelly and colourful and ready-mades fit the bill perfectly. I am a huge fan of the Nutrabaits range of ready mades. To me their Cranberry Classic Combination boilies are ideal for fishing over a mixed seed groundbait and the method is a very effective way to catch carp of all sizes.

I've already pointed out the difference between high attract baits and low attract food baits, and between high quality base mixes and cheaper 50/50 type mixes. Well if you think of ready mades as an attractor bait and use them as and when you would chose an attractor bait rather than a long term food bait, you are half way there.

For instance, I would use a ready-made when stalking observable fish in the margins or when using single hookbaits. AS with oil capsules (see chapter on Hookbaits), on a one bait/one carp basis ready-mades are as good, if not better in terms of attraction than a home made low attract food bait.

I will also use ready-mades if I'm fishing short sessions or guest trips on waters that I know are being pressured by baiting teams using a long term approach. For instance, if four or five guys are putting twenty mixes a week into a lake, I am unlikely to be able to compete with their baiting level or with their bait quality, but I would be confident that I might get a chance or two by offering something completely different from usual fare on offer in the form of a few – not too many – high attract ready-mades.

On the other hand, if I was putting a great deal of time in on the same water as the baiting team, then ready-mades would not be the long term bait of choice. The baiting team may well be swamping the effect of all other bait offerings so in that case I would either try to establish a better bait than theirs (which may very well be mega-hard to achieve) or get on the same team with them!

I also use ready-mades for the majority of my French carp fishing. Why? Because they are convenient, well packaged and preserved and their attractive qualities usually guarantee success, but their main advantage is that they save me loads of time. I usually take between twenty and thirty kilos of finished baits with me to France for a ten-day campaign; imagine the hours I'd have to spend making that little lot at home if I decided to use a proprietary base mix. If you run your own business or are tied down by family commitments making bait is a chore that can well be done without. I know that Kevin would not be able to devote anything like the amount of time to his fishing if he had to make his own baits all the time. There is no getting away from it; ready-mades are a Godsend if you are pushed for time.

However, on waters infested with crayfish or by thousands of tiny American catfish ('poisson-chats'), most ready mades are too soft. You can easily harden them by placing them on Gardner Air-Dry trays for three to four weeks.

Finally I use a ready-made on day-ticket waters for the simple reason that most of these kinds of carp fisheries have seen every permutation of flavour, attractor, base mix and standard of preparation you could possibly imagine and they are so confused as to what to pick up next that I don't think it matters what you use!

College Reservoir is an example of such a water at times. The lake used to be a ready-made only water. Local angler Gary Thomas started a bait company selling inexpensive, but highly effective ready-mades and naturally enough, soon every angler on the reservoir was using Gary's baits. For four or five years it was hard to get a touch if you weren't on Cyprobaits ready-mades, but gradually they began to slow down. More nutritional food baits found favour again and nowadays the water is a Big Fish Mix/Four Seasons Mix water. What comes around goes around.

However, because I like to do something different on hard fished pressure waters such as College, I generally take on the water with Nutrabaits Classic Combination ready-mades on my now rare visits to the water. In 1996 I fished only one three night/four day session for 26 takes – 20 carp on the bank – while in 1997 I again fished only the once and took another twenty carp in three days fishing. Bear in mind that College is a 'bait' water these days, and a hard pressured one at that, yet a bait that most anglers might consider to be ineffective after the hammering the water had on them, cleaned up.

That said, I would most certainly never consider fishing College for a year-long season using ready-mades alone. If I was putting in the sessions on the water I would definitely use a long term approach using a food bait, maybe switching to the ready-mades just once or twice during the year to try and catch them on the hop.

I use my own flavour and attractor combination on base mixes of proven quality whenever I feel that the fish are wised up to bait, especially if the lake is one I intend to fish regularly as opposed to making just the odd visit. For instance, if I was planning on fishing one of the top carp waters in the country such as Withy Pool or the Mangrove I would never consider going in with a ready-made. However, I might very well use one as an alternative hookbait over a carpet of food baits, or as a single hookbait offered in isolation, well away from the main bed of bait.

To achieve success on the hard waters, you need to put in the hours and the bait in equal proportions. I would not even think of going to Savay and sitting behind a thousand ready mades. I believe that way a blank lies. Instead I would use a home made bait in which I had total confidence and over whose production I had complete control. I would then seek to establish this bait as a food source by heavy baiting. In this way a carp would become used to the nutritional properties of the bait and would recognise its food signal whenever it encountered it. I do not believe you can do this with ready-mades. The two baiting applications are as far apart as are the types of bait themselves.

I have only used three makes of ready-mades in my fishing career; Richworths, KM Professional Boilies and Nutrabaits Classic Combination ready-mades. I rate them all very highly but nowadays I tend to favour any ready-made that includes a blend of flavours and/or essential oils and liquid food additive. In

Ready-mades hardening on Gardener Tackle's Air-Dri trays.

terms of attraction these ready-mades are head and shoulders above the cheap and cheerful ready-mades that are based on very low quality ingredients with just a single flavour. These may be all right for a few angling situations, but not for the majority of the ones I find myself in.

Nowadays my favourites are Cranberry and the Cream Cajouser Classic Combination ready-mades from Nutrabaits, but that's just a personal preference. The whole range of six flavours and attractor blends is excellent.

Of the KM Professional range, I think the Honey Necta and the Strawberry Oil Palatant take a lot of beating, while Kevin's own favourites are Ultra Birdspice and Peach Oil Palatant.

14. Making Baits

Making your own baits is simple. Here's how you go about it. First of all you'll need a decent sized saucepan and a well fitting strainer; something like a chip pan and strainer will do nicely. You will need a selection of tough, good sized mixing bowls, and wooden spoons, spatulas and knives for mixing and cutting the paste prior to rolling. Measuring spoons of various sizes are essential for measuring out liquid flavours and attractors. I use a set of kitchen utensils bought specifically for bait making. Most flavours, oils, colours and ingredients smell very strongly and some are heavily pigmented. They can taint and stain plastic and wooden kitchen utensils and I doubt if your wife, mother or girlfriend will take too kindly to you contaminating her best kitchenware with your obnoxious carp tempters!

A cutting board is useful for rolling out bait sausages, but any flat, smooth, washable surface will serve the purpose. However, for the best sausages a rolling table is very useful. Gardner Tackle make an adjustable rolling table that is absolutely outstanding. It rolls sausages from 8mm to 28mm. These bait tables should ideally be complemented with a bait gun which makes the whole process much more efficent and streamlined. The Rolls Royce of bait making equipment comes from Mark Shilham. The Shilham bait rolling table and compressed air-driven bait gun takes 90% of the hard work out of making bait. It's not cheap, but is well worth the money.

You'll also need a hair drier and a supply of either old newspapers, or discarded kitchen or bathroom towels for drying off the finished baits after they come out of the saucepan, and a set of simple kitchen scales for weighing out your ingredients in their correct quantities. Finally some freezer bags for storing the finished baits in the refrigerator or freezer until they are needed.

First break five or six large eggs into a bowl and add the flavour, sweetener and colour and any other attractors as required. Remember not to exceed the recommended level of any attractor or you may end up making a bait that is actually repulsive rather than attractive. You will have to use trial and error to determine the correct number of eggs you will need to use as different base mixes require a variable number. As a general rule of thumb five or six size 2s will cope with 500g of most base mixes. Whisk the eggs, colour and flavouring together thoroughly.

Now it's time to prepare the dry ingredients prior to mixing them with the eggs. Add 500g of either your own mix or any of the excellent proprietary mixes now available to the whisked eggs and flavours and knead until you have a round, fairly stiff ball of dough. You'll find it best to add the dry mix a bit at a time, using the wooden spoon to blend the wet and dry ingredients together. As the mix thickens into a stiffer paste you will have to use your hands rather than the spoon to mix in the last bit of dry powder. You'll know when you have achieved the correct consistency because the ball of paste is easy to knead, and has lost most of its stickiness.

Continue to knead the bait for several minutes, as the longer you do this the easier your baits will be to roll. If you do encounter problems with the paste sticking to your hands, smear them with a vegetable oil.

If you've got a bait-making table or a Rollerball, you now need to make 'sausages' out of the ball of paste, using either the rolling table provided or the extruding bait gun. These are then cut to a length to fit the rolling table. The sausages are then placed on the table 2 or 3 at a time and the baits are produced simply by following the operating instructions supplied. Place the baits on a tray or other flat surface that has been covered with grease-proof paper. Once the whole big ball of dough has been processed the baits are ready for boiling.

If you haven't got a Rollaball you will have to roll the baits in the palm of your hand. With practice you'll be able to make three or four at a time. However, making boiled baits is lot easier with a rolling table and a bait gun so these are worth buying.

20mm Baitmaster Rollaball in use.

Removing baits from boiling water.

Now you are ready to finish off the baits by boiling them. Place about twenty in the strainer and immerse them in boiling water for the required time depending on how hard you want the finished baits to be. The longer you boil them, the harder they'll be which is useful when crayfish or bream are a problem.

Don't put too many baits into the boiling water at once as this will knock the water off the boil. After they have been boiled, put the baits into a colander and apply heat from the hair drier. This drives off the surface moisture. However, the baits will still be warm inside and will sweat if you store them at this point. They need to dry out properly and cool down completely before you can bag and store them.

To do this place the baits onto a Gardner Tackle Air-Dri tray, or clean towel or newspaper. Leave them for at least two hours to cool and dry off completely and then the baits are ready for use. Alternatively you can store the baits by putting them into the freezer. (Remember to label the bag with the date the baits were made and the flavour that was used.)

Boiled baits don't necessarily have to be round. We only make them that shape so that they will go a long way out of a catapult or throwing stick. If you are fishing the margins or at fairly short ranges of up to about 40 metres you don't need to roll the baits into balls at all. In fact, in rivers round baits could even be a drawback as the flow tends to take them out of the baited area.

For quick and easy boiled shapes I just boil the cut up sausages as they are, without either using a Rollerball or shaping them into round baits. Alternatively you can make sausages that fit into the pan, and boil the sausage complete. The finished boiled sausage can then be cut to whatever size you require. This is particularly good for making mini-sized boiled baits. The very thin sausage shape is

Boiled then chopped 'sausages'.

boiled for about 40 seconds and chopped into tiny pieces with up to 1500 particle sized boiled baits from a 500g mix.

Here's yet another method of making up your baits. It is called "Bricking" and is ideal for anyone who uses large quantities of bait as many mixes can be made in a bait-making session. The finished product isn't like ordinary round balls of a uniform size, but comprises hundreds of small cubes of differing densities that are perfect if baiting up from a boat, when fishing the margins, or in rivers. The instructions are as follows:1) Make up the large ball of dough as described above, then knead and shape the bait into a brick shape approximately 8cm x 8cm x 16cm in size.2) Wrap the brick tightly in cling film and place the brick inside a polythene bag. Suck as much air as possible out of the bag then totally submerge the brick in a large pan of boiling water and simmer for one hour. You'll find that any section of the brick not submerged during the boiling will end up as a floating bait so place a weight of about a pound on top of the brick to keep it completely submerged during the boiling.3) After an hour remove the brick from the pan and cut away the polythene and cling film and allow the cooked brick of bait to cool.4) Your bait can now be cut into cube shapes to any size you require. Baits from the outer crust will be semi-buoyant so keep them separate and use them as balanced hookbaits.

Of course, if you want to present a bait in its most natural state you can fish the boilie mix as a paste. You just make up the bait as if you were going to make boilies but stop as soon as the large paste ball is formed. Store the paste in a polythene bag and take it fishing – simple! All base mixes can be fished in this manner, and I have found that pastes of fishmeal mixes are particularly effective.

The advantages that paste baits have over boilies is that the flavour can leak out more quickly. Also, as no heat has been applied, the natural state of the ingre-

Bait expert, Bill Cottam with a glorious 30 pounder.

Kevin Maddocks
Carp Rods

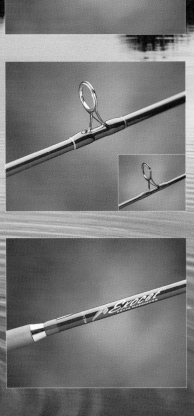

Built for the next Millennium

he history of the Kevin Maddocks carp rods is legendary. The first carbon carp rods in the world carried the
M marque and immediately they became Europe's most successful range. Now twenty years on, you are once
ain offered an amazing range of rods, a range that has no competition, a range designed for the 21st
ntury......

'e were spoilt for choice, as we scrutinised rod blanks worldwide, only one survived our rigorous tests. It was
en lavished with the finest cosmetics ever seen on a carp rod. So step into the future, today, and treat yourself
the world's finest carp rods.

The Blanks: handmade in Britain exclusively for this range - the slimmest and lightest of their type
ywhere in the world.

The Rings: all models feature attractive double-leg frames finished in polished gunsmoke. Challenger™
odels are available with 'gold' or gunsmoke Hp Zo² centres. Exocet™ and Silurus™ models have gunsmoke Hp
o² centres.

The Collars: five, precision-turned steel collars; highly polished nickel on extreme-range Exocet™ models
d 'gold' or nickel on Challenger™ models. A touch of class!

The Handle: unique Fuji/KM reel fitting on Challenger™ and Exocet™ models. Custom-built with
tended nut and beautifully finished with metal collars at each end.

The Butt Grip: tough E.V.A. grip in dark grey (colour co-ordinated with reel fitting), terminated with
atching turned metal collar and butt cap (nickel or 'gold').

The Finishing Touches: beautifully hand crafted in Britain. Smooth, high gloss finish in fabulous
ightfire Red on Exocet™ and Chestnut Brown on Challenger™. Unique identification labels. Matching steel
-inforcement collar on over-fit top joint, tightly-whipped carbon line clip and two neoprene rod bands on all
rp models.

The Carp Series

11.5'	1.75lb	KM Challenger	£230.00
12'	2.25lb	KM Challenger	£235.00
12'	2.75lb	KM Challenger	£240.00
12.5'	3.00lb	KM Challenger	£250.00

Extreme Range Models

12.5'	3.50lb	KM Exocet	£265.00
13'	3.75lb	KM Exocet	£275.00

The Catfish Series

11'	3.00lb	KM Silurus	£185.00
11'	3.50lb	KM Silurus	£195.00
9.5'	4.00lb	KM Silurus	£185.00
8'	5.50lb	KM Silurus	£195.00

ilurus™ models are finished in a dark green criss-cross wrap with full length duplon handle incorporating a 20mm Fuji FPS reel fitting.

BEEKAY
INTERNATIONAL

Withy Pool, Henlow Camp, Bedfordshire SG16 6EA.
Tel: 01462 816960 Fax: 01462 817253

dients is maintained. Proteins, carbohydrates, salts, sugars and fats are all denatured by prolonged heat, so by fishing the paste un-boiled you have got a much more nutritious bait with a far stronger food signal.

To fish pastes you can either simply mould it around the hook, or you can fish it on a hair rig. Just thread a small plastic bead onto the hair loop and mould the paste around the bead.

The main disadvantages of paste baits are that they also attract nuisance fish and small roach and bream will make short work of very soft pastes. Even harder textured pastes will not withstand the attentions of small fry for too long. Also, due to their softer nature, paste baits will not withstand any amount of long range casting effort or the use of heavy leads.

Finally, here are just a few general points that need to be remembered when you are making your own baits at home.

Pungent, unnatural smells such as cigarettes, and carp baits do not go together. If you are a smoker, as I am, make sure your hands are clean and no taint of cigarettes lingers on them. The same applies to other odours such as soap, petrol or engine oil.

Clean the cooking and mixing utensils thoroughly after use. You may think that they are only going to be used for making baits for stupid fish that aren't worried about kitchen hygiene, but bacteriological contamination may make your baits absolutely useless due to unhygienic procedures.

Make sure the baits are completely cold before putting them into the bag ready for the freezer. Warm baits cause condensation to form on the inside of the bag which turns to ice and 'burns' the baits during freezing. For the same reason

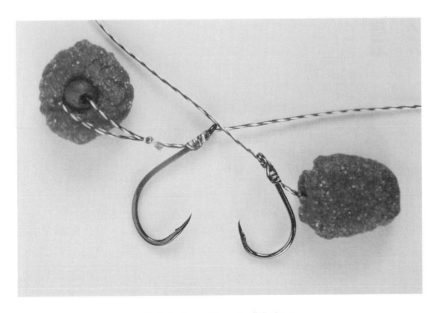

Paste baits and how to fish them.

make sure you draw as much air as possible from the bag before you seal the bag and pop it in the freezer. A very useful item is a heat sealer, which forms a neat air tight seal on polythene bags.

You can keep baits for quite long periods out of the fridge or freezer, but remember that the enemy of all boilies is dampness or atmospheric moisture. A handful of uncooked long grain rice, added to a bag of boilies, will absorb quite large quantities of moisture and keep the baits in good condition, but for long term preservation you will need to add a preservative of some kind. Nutrabaits' Preservabait and the KM Perfector Shelf-Life Preserver are two products which enable you to extend the life of home produced boilies.

15. Hookbaits

Depending on the kind of water you are fishing, you may need to draw attention to your hookbait in some way. Many of the hard-pressured waters contain carp that are wily beyond belief and over the years many weird and wonderful schemes have been hatched to try to get under their guard. Several of these have involved making the hookbait stand out from the surrounding free offerings.

There are several ways in which you can do this; either by making it smell different or by making it behave in a different fashion, or simply by placing additional baits tight to the hookbait in order to make the carp less wary.

The simplest form of hookbait is a standard bottom bait. As its name suggests this is no more than an ordinary bait chosen at random from all the others just like it nestling in the bottom of your bait box. It has no added smell, no added buoyancy and is attached to the hair on its own. It is fished without a stringer and to all intents and purposes it is a free offering attached to the hair!

PVA stringers draw attention to the single hookbait by presenting four or five separate baits in close proximity to the hookbait. As you will probably know, PVA is a soluble material that can be formed into lengths or strings. Standard bottom baits are threaded onto the PVA string, then attached to the hook. When in the water the PVA melts and leaves the baits tight to the hookbait. This makes it more difficult for a wary carp to identify the hookbait.

Hookbaits comprising two standard bottom baits are a natural progression. Carp become used to seeing single offerings on the lake bed, and after a time may well become suspicious of them. But they suffer from tunnel vision: to a blinkered carp often a single bait spells danger; two baits lying together are therefore perfectly safe! By adding two standard bottom baits to a hair instead of one, the carp may well be fooled for a time.

Next, the so-called snowman rig. This too is a double bait presentation but here the bait nearest to the hook is a standard bottom bait, while the one nearest to the boilie stop is a buoyant bait (we'll look at how to make these in a moment). The buoyant bait is supported by the weight of the standard bottom bait so the rig sits nicely on the bottom with the upper bait wafting enticingly in the current.

You can add bouyancy to the hookbait by adding either cork balls or polystyrene inserts. Cork balls are the most bouyant. They come in various sizes so you can control the amount of bouyancy you build into your hookbait. But why should you want to do this is the first place, you ask?

Try this simple experiment. Run 50cm of cold water into the bath and place a dozen or so baits on the bottom. Now take a standard bottom bait presentaion, including the hooklink, swivel, weight and mainline and place it among the other baits. Immitate the action of a carp swimming slowly through the area with a gentle wave of your hand over the baits and the hookbait. Note how the free offerings are more affected by the current you have created than is the hookbait. If you can notice it, the carp can notice it too! After a while they can get so spooky of a bait that behaves differently to the free offerings that they steer clear of it.

By adding bouyancy you can: a) either make your hookbait behave in the same way as the free offerings. This is called a balanced bottom bait, or: b) actually make your hookbait stand up off the bottom to make it more accessible to the carp. This kind of bait is called a pop-up.

This book is about bait, not rigs or tactics, so the merits or otherwise of each strategy you will have to deduce for yourself, depending on the water you are fishing. If you are uncertain the whole subject is clearly explained in the Beekay Guide to Carp Rigs by Kevin Maddocks and Julian Cundiff. Here's how to make both types of buoyant bait.

Cork balls are available in several different sizes. Obviously the bigger the ball, the more buoyant it is. I recommend 10mm and 15mm cork balls from Gardner Tackle. Both buoyant bottom baits and pop-ups are made by forming an outer coating of your boilie mix around the cork ball, so after you have formed the majority of your free offerings, keep a small quantity of boilie mix on one side. To make a pop-up bait, take a 15mm cork ball and mould around it a thin outer coating of boilie mix. Squeeze the resulting bait hard between the palms of your hands so as to compress the paste around the cork ball as much as possible. Then boil the resulting baits for about half the time as you would boil the standard free offerings. You only need a fraction of the boiling time as you are not trying to harden the bait right through, only the outer skin surrounding the cork ball. Once the baits have been boiled dry off the surface moisture with a hair dryer then place them on a drying rack, clean towel or piece of newspaper to dry. REMEMBER TO KEEP TREATED HOOKBAITS SEPARATE FROM THE FREE OFFERINGS!

To make a balanced bottom bait repeat the process using a 10mm cork ball. Whereas the larger cork ball provides enough buoyancy to require some sort of added counter balancing material such as split shot or tungsten putty, the smaller cork ball should only provide enough buoyancy to counteract the weight of the hook. You can test this is a glass of water. Pop the bait in the water. It should sink about half way towards the bottom then slowly rise to the surface again. Now attach the bait to your rig and hooklink and re-test. The baited rig should now sink slowly until the hook lies flat on the bottom and the bait is suspended on the hair above the hook. If the hook is too light, or you have put too much paste around the bait prior to boiling, the bait will be too buoyant to go to the bottom with just the weight of the hook. If this should happen try moulding a tiny bit of tungsten putty around the shank of the hook. You can add more putty or take some off to achieve a bait that is critically balanced with practically neutral buoyancy.

Polystyrene inserts act in much the same way as cork balls. However, they are available in a much wider range of sizes and are ideal for making a variety of different sized hookbaits with varying degrees of buoyancy.

I have outlined the above simply to give you ideas for a presentation that may work for you on the water you are fishing: personally I use either standard bottom baits or balanced buoyant bottom baits for all my fishing. I particularly like using ready-made pop-ups from the Nutrabaits and KM Professional ranges. The floating version of the KM Donkey Chokers are exactly that! 25mm of buoyant pop-up bait that is geared towards attracting, then catching big carp.

The Nutrabaits Classic Combination Pop-ups are ideal for Snowman rigs.

They come in two sizes and are matched to the range of standard flavours. I like the Cream Cajouser versions best of all. A 20mm standard bottom bait is used to counter-balance the buoyancy of the 20mm ready made pop-up. Packs of specially made Snowman hookbaits are available in the KM range as ready-made baits.

You can draw attention to your hookbait in other ways too. Adding extra flavour by way of bait soaks and sprays adds instant attraction to the hookbait, making it stand out from the free offerings by its extra smell. Take care not to overdo the strength of the spray or dip, as we have already discussed the effect of excessive flavour levels around a hookbait (see chapter 4).

I make my own soaks and bait sprays based upon Nutrabaits Multimino-PPC. I invariably use more or less the same recipe for both spray and soak, the recipe being as follows:

65ml Multimino-PPC
20g Betain HCL (dissolved in the Mutimino-PPC)
25ml Pure Salmon Oil
10ml flavour (the same flavour that is in the baits).

The Kevin Maddocks Hookbait Enhancer Dips are some of the very best on the market.

I place the mixture in a 100ml flavour bottle, then attach an atomiser spray for extra versatility.

Hookbait enhancer dips have become all the rage lately. Some of the very best come from the Kevin Maddocks stable. There is a complimentary hookbait enhancer for every flavour in the KM range and you simply soak your hookbaits in the Hookbait Enhancer of your choice for up to 24 hours, depending on the strength of attraction you are looking for. I find hookbait dips are at their best in winter when the carp are not likely to be very active. The extra smell may just be enough to stir a lethargic carp from its winter idlesness to investigate the alluring smell.

Most commercial products are made by adding solvent to a flavour along with other proven attractors such as Minamino. I do not recommend using neat flavour as a soak as this will be too strong: hence the use of added solvent to dilute the strength of the flavour.

Dips consisting of neat fish oil are very effective; you can even add a few drops of essential oil or flavour to the fish oil to add to the attraction.

My favourite bait soak is neat Multimino-PPC. I know I go on about this product but it really is one of the best all-round attractors there is. For a long term soak, add 25-50ml of Multimino to a suitable container then add your hookbaits. Seal the container and shake well. Then leave the baits to stand until required. What could be easier?

Bait sprays are available from a number of bait firms. They are usually purpose-designed to compliment a particular type of bait. Once again I find these work best of all during the winter months. Some bait sprays are water-based, so obviously it's NOT a good idea to use a hookbait spray if you are attaching a stringer or tying the hookbait to the shank of the hook with PVA. If you spray, the

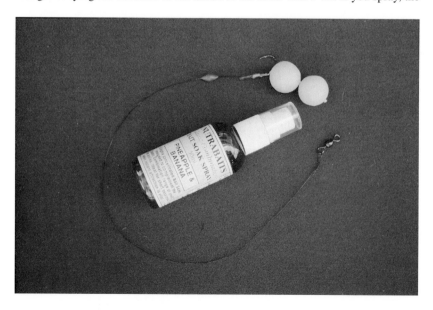

Bait spray and a Snowman rig.

PVA will melt before you can get around to casting out...if it's good PVA, that is!

I have to admit that I am not too keen on over-flavoured hookbaits, but I seem to find myself fishing for ultra-cautious carp these days. One tactic worth trying – and it takes a bit of bottle to do so on big waters – is to use single hookbaits. No free offerings, no stringer, no nothing, just the hookbait. In a one bait/one carp situation I always feel that extra attention needs to be paid to the smell of the single offering. Actual nutrition, as such, doesn't come into it. The SMELL of food, yes. The food value itself, no.

Finally, you can draw attention to your hookbait by using a dissolving pellet or oil capsule. This can be attached to the lead, as with the Richworth Attracta Leads, or placed on the hair, or even buried within the bait. Here are some ideas you may like to try using dissolving oil capsules.

My prefered capsules are garlic oil pearls and cod liver oil capsules. I am also very excited by the reaction I have observed from carp when they catch the smell of Oil of Evening Primrose Capsules. I have seen carp turning underwater somersaults in the presence of this oil and while I have no idea what it is that turns them on, something obviously does.

I used to gear the type of capsule I used to the type of hookbait but now I don't bother. I think all three are equally effective at times and I have even used one of each on a hair. I call this presentation Ken's Full House! It works, honest!

I fish oil capsules in one, or more of the following ways.

First as an addition to the bait on the hair. Simply pierce an oil capsule with a fine needle and thread it onto the hair before the hookbait. What could be simpler? As soon as the baiting needle punctures the capsule it begins slowly to leak its contents in the vicinity of the hookbait.

Secondly as a hookbait in its own right. This is a pure attractor bait and a

Some of the best oil capsules.

How to fish a single capsule with a standard boilie.

method that is pretty self-explanatory. It is best suited to stalking methods for visible fish as the capsules will melt fairly quickly once immersed in water and you don't want to be fishing with a bare hook! However, if fishing with capsules as a bait has never been tried on your local water, give it a try. It can be very instant and at times give superb results. You may need to recast every fifteen to twenty minutes to be certain your hookbait is still intact. I have found that the warmer the lake water the quicker the capsules dissolve.

Incidentally, two capsules of cod liver or Evening Primrose Oil are just bouyant enough to lift a size 6 Penetrator Series 3 hook off the bottom, but as the oil slowly leaks out, the capsules gradually loose bouyancy. For a short time, when the amount of oil left in the capsule exactly counter-balances the weight of the hook, the hookbaits hover enticingly in a state of almost perfect neutral bouyancy.

Ken's Full House Rig using three oil capusles

Finally, try fishing the oils inside the hookbait. This is a more long term method of drawing attention to the hookbait as the oil capsule is not directly exposed to the water. Simply place a capsule in the centre of what will become your hookbait and boil in the normal way. It's as if you were making cork ball pop-ups, substituting the cork ball for the oil capsule. It is very easy to form boile paste around the oil capsule. Why not mould a fishmeal boilie mix around a garlic oil capsule, or try birdfood paste around a cod liver oil capsule or a protein HNV paste around an Evening Primrose Oil capsule?

As soon as the hookbait is pierced by a baiting needle, the oil capsule is also penetrated. The oil from the insert immediately begins to leak out in minute droplets.

For the best of both worlds try adding a couple of oil capsules to the hair and then thread on a hookbait that has had a capsule buried inside it. This way you get an instant leak of attractor from the exterior capsules, and a longer period of release from the interior one. Clever, eh?

$31^{1}/_{2}$ pounds (14.3kg) of deep-bodied mirror for Ken.

16. Groundbait and Mass Baits

There is nothing new about using groundbait to attract coarse fish into your swim. Match and pleasure anglers have been doing it for decades, even for centuries, but groundbaiting for carp?

I have to say that for most of my 30 years in carp fishing I have been trailing along in the wake of most modern carp angling techniques, but I think I can say with some pride that I was one of the first UK carp anglers to pioneer the use of groundbait and its closely related technical cousins, boilie crumb and boilie soup.

Of course, my experiments were cribbed from French anglers who are past masters at the art of formulating and applying mass baiting techniques for carp fishing. I was fishing a Brittany lake in 1988 when I first saw an angler deliberately baiting his swim with loose feed with the aim of not just attracting all coarse fish into his swim, but carp in particular. I brought the idea back home with the intention of applying it on Savay with my friend and fellow rota member, Bill Speed, but though we talked the nights away exploring the ins and outs of groundbaiting on Savay, the consensus of opinion was that all we'd get in the swim were bream; thousands of 'em!

As it turned out, we even got the bream bit wrong. I tried piling in a mass of groundbait – mainly breadcrumbs – for a session in Wilson's in 1989 but I blanked and put the idea onto the back burner to simmer for a while.

We move on a year. Back in Cornwall the carp in Salamander had started playing hard to get. I pulled the idea back to the front of the cooker and took it to the lake. In fact, I'd been inspired by an early programme in John Wilson's 'Go Fishing' series. John had been fishing for tench using a much more sophisticated groundbait than mere breadcrumbs so I took a stroll around the farm supply warehouses and eventually put together a mix consisting of equal parts groats, crushed hemp (from J.E. Haith), Salmon Fry Crumb (BP Nutrition) and maize meal. I made up a big sack of the dry mix and began introducing it in a particular swim on Salamander on a regualr basis. The dry mix was mixed with lake water and a tin of evaporated milk, then left to stand for 24-36 hours until the bucket began to fester a bit.

I began fishing after a week's heavy baiting and was almost immediately into carp. In the space of a few short sessions I was rewarded with a string of good fish including all five twenties in the lake and nineteen of their buddies, out of a total of just thirty-two carp then present in the entire lake. Not bad, I thought to myself. I've been a groundbait fan ever since.

Nowadays there are specialist carp groundbaits galore including Richworth's

Carp XL Plus, Hinder's A Mix and the latest addition to the market, Nutrabaits' Specialist Carpet Feed. This is a fabulous mix that is far more than just another groundbait. It is a delicate blend of crushed hemp, crushed seeds, alfalfa, hemp cake, crushed rapeseed, crushed human grade peanuts and that all-time biggie, Betaine Hydrochloride. It contains no breadcrumbs whatsoever and its inherent oil content means that the dry mix requires very little liquid compared with other more traditional groundbait mixes.

By the way, all the groundbaits mentioned above will bind together into balls simply by adding water, flavour, and a liquid food such as Minamino.

Of course, groundbaiting is still likely to attract all coarse species as well as carp and some anglers believe that this reduces, rather than increases, your chances of success. Their argument is that hordes of frantic little fry dashing around like mad things over a carpet of groundbait will actually put carp off the idea of joining in the feast. Perhaps this might be so in the case of very old, very large carp that may well be loners, but I believe that for the majority of carp angling situations, if you can get the swim boiling with feeding fish of all kinds, then carp will inevitably follow their example, out of curiosity, if for no other reason. Indeed, my whole carp fishing strategy these days is based around getting the maximum amount of feeding activity in my swim, and I don't just mean from carp. I realise that I am at odds with the accepted wisdom here but my experience both at home and abroad tells me that carp are naturally inquisitive creatures that are instinctively drawn to any kind of feeding activity.

Though the upsurge in commercially produced groundbaits is bound to continue and more bait companies will jump onto the bandwagon, there are several blended groundbaits that can be as effective as anything the bait companies can offer, and at a fraction of a price!

I have always stated that my favourite recipes are those that require the minimum of preparation. If I am out by the lakeside with a sack of blended dry ingredients, I don't want to be forever boiling this and sieving that in order to achieve a satisfactory result. All the groundbaits I use are prepared either by a soak in water, or at worst by pouring a kettle of boiling water over a bucket full of mix.

I'll give you a couple of recipes that I can almost guarantee will work on any water. The first I developed in conjunction with Bill Cottam and Nige Britton especially for fishing in France. I enjoyed a great deal of success using it on a variety of waters both large and small throughout the country. Surprisingly enough, it also did very well on a number of UK waters and went on to work particularly well at Fishabil during the era of the regular Carpworld-organised trips. It is a simple blend, equal thirds of the following ingredients:

Oat groats (Haith's or farm supply warehouses)
Flaked maize (from farm supply warehouses).
Canary seed mix (Red Band from J.E.Haith, or Partiblend from Hinders).

For a day's fishing it is as well to make up a bit more than you think you will need. You can always bung in any bait left over at the end of the day, it will do no harm. To make five kilos of finished groundbait, you will need three kilos of dry mix. Place this in a suitable container, then add 15-20ml strong fruity flavouring such as Nutrabaits Pineapple or Strawberry Nutrafruit, 50ml of Multimino-PPC or Sense Appeal and for that finishing touch, a 100g jar of false caviar, or lumpfish eggs, which are widely available at most supermarkets. Add water so that the dry ingredients are covered by 40-50cm of water and allow to soak overnight. By the

Oat groats, flaked maize and canary feed; a good groundbait.

next morning the groundbait will be ready to use.

As it stands the mixture will not bind together to form balls, but it can be introduced with a spod, or by hand into the margins, or of course, by boat where this is allowed. If you want to bind the mixture so that it can be formed into balls, simply add a mixture of maize meal and soya flour. Allow the added ingredients to soak in, then mix to a satisfactory consistency. You will find that it is easy to form any size of ball that will catapult well out into the lake. If you are throwing the bait balls out by hand, dampen your palm with lake water first, this will prevent the bait balls sticking to your hand as you throw.

I fish most of the summer months with fishmeal boilies. On their own they are superb, fished over groundbait they are even better. This is a groundbait that I have put together to use in conjunction with Big Fish Mix boilies. Again it is a blend, this time consisting of equal parts:

Oat groats

Crushed hemp (from J.E. Haith)

Red Band (from J.E.Haith)

Salmon fry crumb (from farm shops or BP Nutrition).

Preparation is exactly the same as before, including the false caviar, but this time I spice up the three kilos of dry mix with the addition of 10 grams of Betaine HCl. I also swap the fruit flavour for a savoury one, usually a smelly fish flavour such as Salmon Elite, Lobster Palatant or the fabulous Squid and Octopus Koi Rearer, or the excellent Monster Mussel or Prawn and Shrimp from the KM Liquid Smell range of flavours.

Add water, stir well and allow to soak for 12 hours so that the groats soak up as much liquid as possible. The natural oils from the salmon crumb and the crushed hemp makes this groundbait almost instantly attractive.

MASS BAITS

To all intents and purposes there is little difference between groundbaiting and putting out a carpet of mass baits such as dari seed, groats or boiled hempseed. They work in exactly the same way by encouraging a feeding frenzy of all coarse fish in your swim. Mass baits were really the predecessor of groundbait blends and there are many waters in the UK and abroad where mass baits work very well.

The easiest of all the mass baits to prepare are oat groats. These soak up water well, doubling their size and taking up flavour and other attractors in a superb manner. A bucket of groats needs just an overnight soak to prepare it, but in my opinion groats will benefit from a scalding with boiling water if that is possible. I like to use a mixture of scalded and soaked groats. This produces a blend of textures that carp find particularly attractive. The day before I am due to fish I pour three pints of boiling water over a kilo of dry, flavoured groats. I let the water cool then add a further two kilos of dry groats and more water, then leave the mixture to soak overnight. You will find that the scalded groats tend to go very soft, almost to a mush, at the same time exuding a milky sweet-smelling substance that I am sure carp adore. The groats that have simply been soaked give a slightly more crunchy texture to the mixture.

I have found that the attractiveness of groats will improve the longer they are soaked. If you can leave a bucketful for five or six days, until the liquor in which they are soaking starts to smell slightly 'off', then so much the better.

Most canary seed mixes make brilliant mass baits and groundbaits. Hinder's Partiblend is a good example of a canary seed mix, but to my mind the best canary seed blend is Red Band from the ubiquitous J.E.Haith of Cleethorpes.

Both these seed mixes definitely benefit from a short boil so as to extract the thick gooey glutinous milk that the seeds exude after boiling. It is hard to explain just how much comes out of the seeds but the boiled seeds actually become almost bound together by the goo.

To get the best out of all canary seed mixes you will need a large saucepan, preferably one that the wife, mother or significant other half has cast aside for the dustbin.

Fill the pan with the dry seed mix so that it comes two thirds of the way to the lip. Then pour boiling water over the seeds and bring back to the boil. Cover with a lid and leave the pan on a fairly high heat. You will now need to boil another kettle so that once the boiling water has dropped below the top of the seed level, you can add a bit more so as to cover all the seeds once again. You will be amazed at how much water the cooking seeds will absorb.

Boil for ten minutes, then turn down the heat to a low simmer to reduce the liquid in the pan. After half an hour you will note that all the liquid has either been evaporated or absorbed by the seeds. The resulting bait will now be so glutinous that it will stick to just about anything. It is ready to use now, but if you wish to form bait balls add a small quantity of semolina, breadcrumbs or maize meal to arrive at the correct consistency.

Incidentally, by grinding Red Band or any type of canary seed to a powder in a coffee grinder you obtain an excellent binder for all types of base mix. Use at 25-30% of the total mix for best results.

No look at mass baits would be complete without mentioning hempseed. From the days of Izaak Walton, coarse anglers have known the attractive properties of hemp.

It is at its most deadly when baited on a little-and-often basis, for carp love hemp so much that if you put too much into your swim the carp often become totally preoccupied on the stuff, often ignoring a perfectly good boilie or nut sitting on the top of the carpet of hemp. In fact, so preoccupied can they become, it has been known for anglers to fish a totally unbaited hook over a heavy carpet of hemp! The carp are so busy hoovering up the seeds that they suck in the hook as well. By using a very short, two inch bolt rig the hook usually finds a hold in the mouth as the carp continues to feed, totally unaware of the fact that there is a hook in its mouth!

If you are bold enough to try this method try adding a tiny bit of pop-up foam to the hook so that it stands up off the lead. Do not, under any circumstances, be tempted to use a longer hooklink. Remember, the carp are shovelling hemp towards their throat teeth as if there is a famine about to happen; use a long hook-link and the hook will almost certainly pass beyond the teeth and the inevitable result will be a bite-off.

Hemp comes in many forms, but the natural seed is the most common. To prepare, add one kilo of sugar (I prefer caster or icing sugar) to five kilos of hempseed in a large saucepan – the same one you boiled to buggery when preparing the canary seed! Cover with cold water and bring to the boil. Then turn down to simmer for approximately 20-30 minutes. You can tell when the seed is cooked as the husk splits open to reveal the soft, white shoots. The hemp is now ready to use.

It is easy to get carried away when baiting up with boiled seed so I tend to use a very small feeder so as to restrict the amount of bait I am tempted to introduce. The best feeder I have found is the old-fashioned, original bait dropper designed for use on deep lakes and fast flowing rivers. There are two sizes available – I use the large one – and they work on the principle of a trap-door release once the feeder hits the bottom. I cast a filled feeder about a dozen times, the casts spread out over quite a wide area. The idea is to get the carp searching hard for the seeds but not so hard that they become preoccupied.

Crushed hemp is an outstanding groundbait ingredient that can also be used on its own if required. Crushed hemp is available from farm stores and warehouses, from Hinders of Swindon and from that old favourite of the carp world, J.E. Haith of Cleethorpes.

Though I prefer to add crushed hemp to form a blend with other ingredients, I have used it on its own as a mass bait. It poses the same problems as does hemp seed in that carp often become totally preoccupied by the stuff to the exclusion of all else, so once again, little and often should be the watchword.

It needs no preparation other then the addition of water, but if you want to bind it to form bait balls you will need to add breadcrumbs or soya flour to form a sticky paste. Hemp Oil from Nutrabaits really complements crushed hemp brilliantly. To prepare enough for a session add 50ml of hemp oil, 50ml Multimino-PPC and 200ml of water to two kilos of dry crushed hemp. Add the liquid to the solids and mix thoroughly in a bowl or bucket. Leave to stand overnight. By the morning you should find that the crushed hemp has combined with the oil and other liquids to form a groundbait-type mixture that will compress into bait balls ready for firing from a catapult.

You will need no indication of where your bait has landed: as soon as the bait balls hit the bottom, water permeates their centres and the natural oil content of the hemp, supplemented by the added hemp oil, starts to leak out. In flat calm conditions you will be able to see the oil droplets coming to the surface as minute, bubble-like disturbances. If there is any chop on the surface, the flat spot caused by the leaking oil will show you where the bait carpet is!

Hemp seed in all its forms can be deadly, but I cannot stress enough how easy it is to over-bait with it. There is nothing so frustrating as seeing constant signs of fish in your swim, with no accompanying pick ups.

A carp fishing style all of its own has been developed to take advantage of the carp's natural inquisitiveness towards well formulated groundbaits. It has chosen to call itself – rather pompously, in my opinion – The Method. If memory serves me well, it was invented by John Hofgartner who developed a special type of in-line feeder which has since been adopted by Richworth. Briefly the idea is that you mould groundbait around the specially designed feeder, at the same time burying the hooklink and hookbait within the groundbait. As you can imagine, the presentation confronts the carp with something entirely new and results on many hard pressured waters have been dramatic, to say the least. Though I believe Richworth currently is at the cutting edge of The Method technology and design, other bait companies are not far behind. I particularly like the Essential Products cage feeder design based around that company's Comet leads – a brilliant concept that allows the groundbait-caked lead and feeder to be cast previously unheard-of distances.

At the time of writing, BCSG member Mike Willmott of Essential Products was in the process of finalising a complementary groundbait to use with his special Carpfeeders. These follow a revolutionary concept that has been specially designed for use with Essential Products' own range of in-line leads. By adding weight to the feeder concept, The Method has come bang up to date, offering a bolt-rig style resistance to a taking carp. Previous cage feeder designs are too light for a bolt effect once the groundbait has softened and fallen away from the feeder. In my opinion Mike's idea is set to revolutionise the whole Method idea.

Before I leave the subject, there are two more foodstuffs that are acceptable as mass baits. Actually, I shouldn't call them baits...they are, more accurately, feeds.

Two of the cheapest mass baits are wheat and barley. These can be purchased in bulk and on most waters carp will eat them. I would not recommend them as either groundbaits or as mass baits, but as supplementary feeds on waters with a low productivity of natural food; they are an excellent, cost-effective feed supplement. On the advice of fishery advisor Dr. Bruno Broughton, my local club has used barley as a close-season feed supplement to excellent effect. While not a highly nutritious food, barley kept the carp in our lakes in good condition as we awaited the end of our self-imposed close-season. The first time we tried it we kept feeding right up to the last minute, a BIG mistake. When opening day came along the carp were still stuffed full of barley!

Both wheat and barley should be soaked for 48-72 hours prior to being introduced to the lake. This is to ensure that the grains take on all the water they are likely too before the carp eat them. You can imagine the terrible problems the would result if unsoaked grains were eaten by the carp immediately following introduction. The grains would begin to swell in the carp's gut with disastrous results.

Fish eggs

17. Boilie Crumb and Boilie Soup

I am not going to claim that I was the first to dream up the idea of a bait carpet comprising thousands of minute particles of boiled bait; Rod Hutchinson was experimenting with the idea in the early 80s. However, I am going to claim that I was the first to bring the idea kicking and screaming onto the modern carp scene.

I first experimented with the crumb in 1989 and my results were so special that I began fishing almost entirely on waters where I knew that the crumb could be effectively introduced.

In 1990 I had a stack of fish from both Salamander Lake and Wheal Rashleigh through baiting a selection of marginal swims with crumb then actually watching the carp go mad on the presentation. So convinced was I of the effectiveness of the method that I wrote about it in the 1990/91 Nutrabaits catalogue. The resounding silence that greeted my pearls of wisdom dented my confidence not one iota; if they want to ignore a brilliant carp fishing method, I thought to myself, then sod 'em!

Of course, the thinkers in the bait world soon got stuck into the idea and now it has been refined and the production process streamlined. These days it is possible to make a truly devastating crumb in a matter of minutes, and with a few bits and pieces added to the finished crumb, the method is probably one of the most effective ways of catching carp.

Let us start with a brief look at how to make a standard crumb. First of all you need to make the basic bait which will eventually be turned into crumb. Alternatively you can take baits that have already been rolled, boiled and frozen; thaw out the baits and process them whole. Alternatively you can make an excellent boilie crumb by processing ready-mades. As we will see in a moment, there are two ways of forming crumb and either will work well with rolled and boiled home made boilies or with ready- mades.

However, if you are going to set out to make a lot of boilie crumb you will probably find that the following method of preparing the basic bait is perfectly adequate.

First take 500g of your chosen base mix or recipe. For best results I prefer slightly coarse birdfood mixes or top quality fishmeals. Add the dry mix to the beaten eggs, flavour and attractors as normal so as to form a paste. Next form 'sausages' from the paste. The exact length and diameter is not important. All you have to remember is not to make them so long that they will not fit into your boiling pan.

Bring the pan of water to the boil and add three or four sausages to boil for two minutes. Do not boil so many at a time that the water comes off the boil. Remove the boiled sausages from the water and dry them off using a hair drier. Process all the sausages in this way, then allow them to harden slightly and cool by leaving them on a towel or newspaper for at least an hour. While you are waiting you can prepare another kilo or two of base mix.

Once the baits have cooled you are ready to make the crumb.

As I mentioned earlier, there are two ways of doing this. The first is to feed the 'sausages' through a food processor – not the one the wife uses for making the spaghetti sauce! This gives a very fine crumb with a soft, delicate texture.

The second method is to feed the sausages through a hand-turned meat mincer, such as a Spong Mincer. These are not that popular with housewives these days, but if you can find one second hand or at a car boot sale or something, you will be well pleased with the results they give.

To make the crumb just cut the boiled sausages into manageable segments and feed them through the meat mincer. Usually the mincer comes with a choice of three cutting discs and obviously the finer the disc you use, the fluffier and lighter is the crumb. I generally use the medium disc to process the majority of my crumb.

As it stands, the crumb is now ready to be used but there are one or two little tweaks you can add to give it still more pulling power. I mentioned false caviar, or lumpfish eggs before. They are a superb ingredient to add to any boilie crumb, boilie soup or groundbait and I really cannot stress how highly I rate them.

Add a 50g or 100g jar of either the red or the black eggs to 500g of processed crumb and its attraction increases considerably. Alternatively you could add a handful (no more) of crushed tiger nuts or peanuts to the crumb.

As it now stands the crumb will not go far from a catapult, in fact, it will probably all come back in your face if there is any onshore breeze! However, you can make up small catapult-sized balls of crumb by dampening the mixture using an atomiser spray consisting of one part water to one part liquid food additive. I use Multimino-PPC, but you can use whatever liquid food you like. You can even add neat flavour to the atomiser spray if you like, but take care not to get too over-enthusiastic as you may defeat the object by putting in too much.

For a day's fishing I generally introduce a complete mix of crumb into my chosen swim, topping this up with half a mix after every fish. If you get the sort of action I have experienced in the past, you may well need half a dozen mixes! Don't go mad with the free offerings. I have had my best results by fishing single hook-baits over the top of the crumb. At the most use no more than two or three bait stringers. Properly made and applied crumb brings the fish on in a big way and they should be heavily on the bait. Too many baits over the top can actually cause them to loose their preoccupation. Then they will pause, suddenly see that they are confronted with a familiar situation that often spells danger – loads of round boilies – and may well spook off the bait. So keep your free offerings to the minimum or fish hookbaits only.

My all-time favourite recipe for the sausages is as follows:

500g Big Fish Mix
20ml Multimino-PPC
15ml Salmon Oil
1ml Sweet Cajouser
8ml Caviar flavour

12 drops Black Pepper essential oil
2g Green Lipped Mussel Extract
4g Betaine Hydrochloride.
Add eggs, roll into 15mm sausages and boil for 75 seconds to two minutes.
Then process as desired (I prefer to use the hand cranked meat mincer).

A natural progression on from boilie crumb is boilie soup. Even as I was
developing the crumb, I realised that carp would, in time, become wise to the ploy,
so I began looking for something even more whacky to try and keep one jump
ahead. The answer I came up with was boilie soup.

Carp find boilie soup incredibly attractive. I have watched them literally
tearing up the bottom to try to find the source of the smell that has drawn them into
the swim. Of course, they cannot find a really tangible mouthful to get their teeth
into and once I've described how I make the soup, you'll understand why. Boilie
soup is easy to make. All you need are some basic ingredients, flavours and attractors, a bucket, some water and a Cobra Groundbaiter baiting spoon.

This is my favourite recipe for the soup:
1kg Big Fish Mix
1kg Yellow Semolina
50ml Pure salmon Oil
20ml Cranberry Nutrafruit
50ml Nutramino
8g Betaine HCl
200g jar of black lumpfish eggs
Put the Betaine HCl, the Green Lipped Mussel Extract, the fishmeal base mix
and the semolina in a big bucket and mix them all together. Now take the liquids
and pour then over the mixture of dry products. Finally, add water to the bucket to
form a wet, sloppy mixture that will pour from one container to another with the
consistency of very runny porridge. That's all there is to it!

In its present form, the soup is probably at its most attractive, but if you wish
to make it go further, at the same time adding a more solid food aspect to the soup,
you can include 250-300g of soaked and boiled oat groats to the soup.

Of course, you don't need to use an expensive base mix such as the Big Fish
Mix to form the base for boilie soup, but as in any baiting approach, the better the
ingredients, the better the results. That said, if you would like to try a less expensive recipe then just about any combination of dry ingredients can be used to make
a tempting boilie soup. Bear in mind that there should be some element of both
attraction and nutrition at the heart of the mix. It is for this reason that I use 50%
Big Fish Mix. Using the same attractors at the levels mentioned in the previous
recipe, an alternative dry mix might be:
500g Yellow Semolina
500g Salmon Fry Crumb or ground trout pellets
1kg Maize Meal
Obviously you are now faced with the problem of getting the soup into your
swim, which is where the hard work comes in. If you've got a boat and are allowed
to use it, all well and good, but boats of all kinds are usually banned on most UK
waters. That leaves you with the choice of swimming the bait out (also probably
banned!), going round to the far side and baiting the unfished margins, or fishing
under your feet. Personally I favour the latter and now perhaps you can see why I
need the Cobra spoon.

Nutrabaits Hemp Pellets – before.

This very handy tool can be screwed into the end of a landing net handle to form a very useful piece of equipment for baiting up. These days I use a three-section extending handle which I bought in Holland, but there are similar extending handles available in the match fishing sections of the bigger tackle shops. Mine extends from six to fifteen feet which gives me ample reach for baiting up the kinds of marginal swims I like to fish.

I have also experimented with the Water's Edge Particle Baiter and I can achieve a reasonable distance with this, provided the soup is not too sloppy. However, I really prefer working with very wet boilie soup so for me the Cobra Groundbaiter is preferable.

To bait up all you do is fill the spoon with soup and stretch it out over the water to the area you have chosen to fish. Lower the spoon so that water slops over the edge. You will note that the soup immediately starts to mix with the lake water and flow out of the spoon. Now gradually turn your wrist so that the spoon slowly empties into the lake. You can sweep the spoon across an arc to spread the soup out or simply dump the whole spoonful in one place. The soup diffuses into the water quickly, then spreads out in an enticing fine layer, filtering down through the water to the lake bed. As soon as the soup mixes with the lake water, the flavours, oils and attractors begin to spread across the bottom.

The big difference between soup and crumb is that the crumb has a more tangible element of food about it, whereas the soup leaves only an ever-widening, frustratingly intangible layer of miniscule food particles on the bottom. There is the enticing smell and taste of food, but nothing for the carp to really get their teeth

The Hemp Pellets – after.

into. It drives them mad! A hookbait offered on a fairly simple presentation stands a very good chance of getting a take.

Carp usually become very active once they get the smell of the soup in their noses, often tearing about the swim as they try in vain to get a proper mouthful. I have often watched as they turned previously gin-clear water a thick, muddy brown with their constant activity.

I believe both crumb and soup work on the frustration principle, particularly where lots of carp are feeding in the swim, competing for what their senses tell them is a spreading carpet of solid food, which does not appear to be borne out in reality. You can picture the scene underwater as the frantic and frustrated carp search more and more actively for tiny morsels of food. The more they search the more they plough up the bottom, fanning the lake bed with their pectorals and tails, their angry activity spreading the enticing smell of food ever wider about the swim. As their frustration grows their caution weakens until they are reduced to grabbing at just about anything solid that looks and smells like food; and that should be your hookbait.

I'm sure that you don't need me to tell you of the obvious drawback to both crumb and boilie soup. In the case of the crumb, it doesn't go far fired from a catapult, while the situations where you can use the soup are limited to margin fishing or baiting up from a boat. Even when fished in a more conventional manner, bound together with a small quantity of soya flour and breadcrumbs and fished as a groundbait, both methods are somewhat restricting, and those very restrictions can detract from the originality of both approaches in some anglers' eyes.

This is a pity and I would urge you to examine the waters you are on and the range at which you are fishing and ask yourself if you are not being rather stereotyped in your approach. If the honest answer is, yes, then I can strongly suggest either boilie crumb or boilie soup as an excellent alternative way of tackling the lake. Suspicious carp in hard-fished waters are often quickly and easily fooled by the uniqueness of these methods.

18. Pellets and Ball Pellets

In the previous two chapters we discussed the effectiveness of the groundbait approach using either a purpose designed groundbait such as The A Mix from Hinders, or Nutrabaits Specialist Carpet Feed, or by creating a feeding situation with a carpet of tiny seeds, groats, boilie crumb or boilie soup. We saw that the only limitations of this type of baiting strategy is that fact that it can only be applied in the margins or from a boat. In an ideal world what is needed is some way of introducing the groundbait principle without being too restricted as far as range is concerned; a dry product that can be introduced by spod, PVA bag or throwing stick, which is where ball pellets and the like come in.

I guess ball pellets are just about the ultimate progression on the groundbait theme to date...and hasn't that come a long way? Never in my wildest dreams did I ever think when I first started messing around with groundbait of various kinds that the concept would be refined to the state-of-the-art techniques around today.

First off, ball pellets, crumb-balls, call them what you will, all work on the same basic principle. At the time of writing there are now four bait companies making their own dissolving 'boilies'. These are Nutrabaits, Solar, Mainline and Nashbaits; others may well be poised to follow their example. From personal experience I can only talk about the Nutrabaits versions but I feel sure that other versions will be equally effective.

Ball pellets are in effect egg-free round balls of bait ingredients combined with powdered flavours, sweeteners, liquid food attractors and other products. The round balls shapes are formed by steam-compressing the powders to form solid balls. When immersed in water the pellets break down within about half an hour to form a little pile of groundbait on the lake bed.

Obviously ball pellets have huge advantages over ordinary boilies, particularly on hard fished waters where the carp are wary of all round balls of bait. Imagine a carpet of mixed ball pellets and boilies on the lake bed; a combination of two thirds ball pellets, one third boilies. The carp is now confronted with a swim a third full of solid, edible bait and two-thirds full of dissolving pellets in varying stages of breakdown. As the carp feed, or attempt to feed, on the pellets the tiny particles are distributed about the swim creating yet again that same principle we saw at work when using boilie soup – the smell and taste of food, but nothing to get their teeth into; once again the frustration principle at work.

Ball pellets are tailor-made for fishing in thick weed. Many anglers favour ordinary trout pellets for most of their weedy water fishing, but I believe that, while these are highly effective, on most waters ball pellets work better, particularly on lakes where there are deep pockets and layers of silt. Being very light, the ball pellets do not bury themselves in soft silt, breaking down into the intended mush on top of the silt, forming a source of attraction both visible and detectable by smell and taste.

Ball pellets can be fired from a catapult to a distance of about 60 yards, and from a throwing stick to about 70 yards. If you dampen them very slightly with their water or perhaps Minamino, you can put an extra ten yards on those distances.

I have used ball pellets for a great deal of my 1997 season, both at home and in France, and I think I can honestly say that they were been the primary factor in what was been an outstanding year for me.

For instance, a two-night session on a small French water produced five twenties to 29lb 12oz (13,5kg) and eight upper doubles. All were tempted from a silt filled gully at 65 yards range. In the two nights I introduced six kilos of ball pellets and two kilos of home made caviar-flavoured fishmeals. I found that the trick was to keep the pellets going in at regular intervals, even during the periods when I wasn't getting takes. I tried to introduce the ball pellets every 30 minutes, adding a dozen or so fishmeal boilies every hour. After an initial spell of heavy feeding I lost the fish, but the introduction of another kilo of ball pellets brought them back. The fish were heavily on the bait by the time I had to leave. I'm sure if I could have stayed another 48-hours I'd have more than doubled my result. As it was I was happy as Larry with the fish that I caught.

It was clear that the fish were very turned on by the ball pellets that were in varying stages of breakdown. I had fish crashing out almost continuously for the whole of the session, indicating that they were greatly attracted by the smell and taste of food. The Big Fish Mix boilies were flavour-matched to the ball pellets, which were the caviar version of the Nutrabaits Ball Pellets. As the fish searched for a more tangible mouthful to eat, they came across the similar smelling boilies and these were snapped up without a second look.

I also fished a very weedy water near my home for a couple of sessions in 1997. The weed had become really thick but it was quite easy to find the holes in the weed. I usually put a marker float out to the hole, then fill it up with boilies. I then put the line in the line clip so that I can re-cast to the hole whenever I want. As far as the bait is concerned, I only want to make sure that the actual solid baits and the hookbait lands in the clear spot. I'm not fussed where the ball pellets go. Provided I can get the range I generally spread the ball pellets out all over the swim, not caring if they are in weed or not. Incidentally, I have found that the two thirds ball pellets: one third boiled baits ratio works wherever I take it.

The reason I am not concerned if ball pellets get hung up in weed is because as they dissolve the miniscule particles of bait will spread out among the weed fronds as small fish and carp swim through the weed, attracted by the smell given off by the ball pellets. You can make things too hard for yourself at times, remember!

I try to maintain a steady flow of ball pellets into the general area of my carpet of boilies, baiting up with the throwing stick every half hour or so. After each fish the marker float goes back out until I am sure it is in the clear, then out go more boilies and the hookbait, followed by a heavy baiting with wide spread ball pellets. Hard work, yes, but worth the effort.

I am not usually too bothered about which flavour the dissolving ball pellets are emiting. Indeed, I have done really well using a combination of two or three different flavoured ball pellets. One of my biggest hits of 1997 was a 59 fish catch, taken on an eight day holiday session. The catch included no less than 22 twenties and four thirties. All told I used fifteen kilos of mixed ball pellets and seven kilos of fishmeal boilies, obvious proof that the carp were not bothered about the flavour of the ball pellets.

To me round, boilie-shaped ball pellets are the ultimate groundbait. They fire out to a reasonable distance and then break down on the lake bed. If, like most of us, you are restricted to baiting up from the bank, there is no better way to create a tantalising smell and taste trail in your swim. That frustrating attraction that lowers the carp's guard as they search for a tangible food source.

One other way of creating a baiting situation is with a carpet of pellets. In the past when a carp man talked about pellets you could be sure he was taking about trout pellets. These days there are so many different types of pellet around it is possible to match the pellet to the type of boilie you are using, for instance, hemp pellets can be used in combination with hemp boilies; Nutrabaits Total Hemp Mix and Total Hemp Pellets, for instance.

For the purposes of this section I have decided to lump all non-round pellets together to avoid confusion.

Pellets come in many sizes, from the large 16mm Big Fish Mix pellets from Essex Bait Services, to the tiny 4mm Micromass pellets from Clive Deidrich. Other well known and highly effective pellets include Response Pellets from Mainline, Total Hemp Pellets from Nutrabaits and both Monster Crab and Formula Majic pellets from Hutchinson. Once again they all work on the dissolving food source principle. Some dissolve more quickly than others but it is rare to find a pellet that has not broken down to a mush within an hour. One that seems to stay intact for ever is the Response pellet, though to be fair, these become very soft after twenty-four hours. In a way they are a bit like the non-specific fish pellets that are often sold as Carp Pellets (sic!). These are usually very poor quality pellets with only a small nutritional value, but a high fat and oil content. They were certainly never formulated specifically for carp and they could equally well be fed to sheep or rabbits! They come a poor second to purpose-designed pellets such as trout pellets.

In fact, trout pellets are probably the best type of feed pellet currently available, despite what the bait companies would have you believe. They have an element of nutrition about them, a good smell and a high fat and oil content. In addition they are usually a lot cheaper than many of the pellets on offer from the bait companies.

That said, there are several carp specific pellets that stand out and these are the two pellets from the Hutchinson stable, the Total Hemp Pellets fron Nutrabaits, and the Big Fish Mix Pellet from Essex Bait Services. The latter is 100% pure compressed, reconstituted BFM, by the way, with flavours and attractors spray-dried onto the pellets for maximum leak-off effect.

I have found that the best way to get a lot of pellets into the swim is to use a spod. My favourite is from Gardner Tackle. The only problem with a spod is that you have to take care not to put too much bait in. As with ball pellets I think that a little-and-often approach is better than piling it in. Obviously if you are fishing the margins up to about twenty yards out, you can use a catapult to put the pellets out, but once again, be wary of putting too much in.

Dissolving pellets attract in exactly the same way as groundbait, mass bait, crumb, soup or ball pellets, that old frustration principle at work again. Pellets that do not breakdown are regarded by the carp as individual food items. It is easier to get a degree of pre-occupation on these pellets, but it is also all to easy to fill them up with them as well. If a carp can actually eat the pellet, as opposed to being attracted by it but only being able to snatch at a few micro crumbs, its hunger will be more quickly satisfied. It follows therefore that quickly dissolving pellets in form a more attractive, more frustrating bait carpet.

As with ball pellets there are several sprays and the like that are designed to complement the pellets. These are a much better option than simply dousing dry pellets with neat flavour. It is possible to over-flavour pellets and thus mess up the attraction effect you are trying to create. Remember, flavours can become carp repellers when used at excessive levels. By using a purpose-designed pellet spray you can be sure that the bait company has put together the correct blend of flavours and other attractors so that the spray adds to the attractiveness of the pellet rather than masks it.

19. Particles

Maybe it is my imagination but there seems to be far fewer carp being caught on particle baits these days. At the peak of their popularity in the seventies and eighties a great many carp anglers were using a particle bait of some kind, but recently many club and private carp waters have introduced particle bans and this may account for the fall in their popularity.

I believe that the main reason for the decrease in the popularity of particle baits is the growth of the bait industry and the ready availability of really top class ready-mades, boilie-making ingredients, base mixes, flavours and attractors. Nowadays it is possible to make a wide variety of superb boiled baits and, quite simply, particles have become less effective. There is no shadow of doubt in my mind that boilies catch more fish, catch bigger fish and do them good at the same time.

Apart from using a few kilos of cooked maize from time to time when fishing in France, I have not used a particle bait for nearly ten years and quite frankly I doubt if I shall be tempted to do so again. The use of mass baits, pellets, ball pellets and groundbaits in conjunction with well formulated boilies is a far more effective method of catching carp than the use of particle baits.

Frankly I am pleased that the widespread use of particles has lost its popularity. Particles are poor food baits that do the carp little good and I believe that it is important that we, as anglers, give back a little to our quarry in the form of decent, nutritional food baits that compensate them in part for the stress we impose by catching them.

However, as no book on carp baits would be complete without a chapter on particle baits here are a few lines about some of the better ones.

MAIZE

Maize is a bizarre bait. At times carp seem to stuff themselves silly on the little yellow grains. The majority of carp anglers that I encounter who use maize seem to prefer to use it uncooked after a 24 hour soak in flavoured water. In this form the grains are bullet-hard and pass straight through the carp more or less intact. I feel that maize is a hundred times more effective if it is not only soaked for at least 2-3 days, but is also then cooked for about thirty minutes. After this preparation most of the grains split and soften and they are far more palatable.

Maize takes on flavour very well and I have also found that it benefits from the addition of a sweetener of some kind. This does not necessarily have to be an artificial sweetener but could quite easily be ordinary white sugar, icing sugar or caster sugar. On the rare occasions that I use maize in France, I flavour a large bucket of 5 kilos of maize with 20ml Strawberry Nutrafruit and 500g of ordinary sugar. The flavour is added to the sugar which is then dissolved in boiling water which is in turn poured over the maize. I add sufficient boiling water to cover the maize by an inch or so, then leave the grains to soak up the sweetened, flavoured water for 24-72 hours, then I boil the grains for half an hour.

After boiling, return the cooked maize and the water in which they have been boiled to the bucket and allow them to cool. Do not drain off the water as continued soaking will encourage the cooked maize to ferment. The liquor will thicken and the maize will start to leak its attractive sugars. The maize is then at its most effective. I am encountering fewer and fewer waters in France where maize is still effective. For many years it was the bait of choice for most French carp anglers as well as with visiting carp men from all over Europe, but with the enormous growth in the popularity of carp angling in France, the widespread use of maize is proving less and less effective.

On the other hand, maize is not a popular particle bait in the UK and provided the bait is properly prepared and applied, I see no reason why it shouldn't be successful on many British carp lakes. I know that College bailiffs Mark England and Steve Beard have done very well using light carpets of maize on the reservoir.

MAPLES

Along with black-eyed beans, this is the best all round particle bait. It takes flavour and sweetener well, it has a fair nutritional value, it softens nicely after an overnight soak and a 15-20 minute boil, and the carp love it!

I used maples a great deal in the late 70s and early 80s and had a lot of fish on them from a number of waters in the south west. I remember using them at Ockenham Lakes in 1980 and stacking 'em up! Maples didn't have a particularly long life, even on what is generally acknowledged to be a 'hungry' water, but they were effective as a short term bait.

To prepare maples, simply soak them for 8-12 hours and boil them until they begin to soften. This generally takes about fifteen minutes. Do not overcook maples or you will find that they becme too soft. After boiling, strain off the water, then return the cooked maples to a container. They can be used immediately and some anglers swear that hot maples are better than ones that have been left to cool.

Personally I have found that maples are at their best after they start to exude a milky strong-smelling substance. This is apparent after about two to three days. The thick liquid is starch and sugar that the maples give off as they begin to ferment.

TIGER NUTS

The so-called 'ultimate' particle...allegedly! Personally I think they are over-rated. I know that they are banned on a number of waters, and a good thing too, in my opinion. The trouble with tiger nuts is that they are usually an instantly effective bait. They catch from the off and this encourages anglers to introduce increasing amounts in the hope of getting better results. And therein lies the problem: the more you put in, the quicker they stop eating them, and they don't just stop eating the tigers; they seem to stop eating ALL baits!

Tigers are best used in very small quantities. I know when my friends were using them on College they were only taking about a kilo of nuts for a 48-hour

Shaun Hodges tempted this mid-30 (16kg) using tiger nuts over Hinders
Hemp/Groundbait

session. They used no more than one or two pouchloads around each hookbait and
only topped up the swim after a take. They did no prebaiting and if they had no
action would take any remaining bait back home with them. In all, four guys used
less than 10kg between them in the course of an entire summer campaign. By
keeping the amount of bait to a minimum they were able to make sure the bait had
a long catching life on the water.

It would have lasted even longer had it not been for the fact that, once others
noted the success of tigers, they too started to use the bait. Soon just about everybody was on them, and the majority were not as conservative in their baiting strategy as my friends. I heard of one guy who put a fifteen kilo bucket of tigers into
his swim at the beginning of a week-long session, then wondered why he blanked.
Tigers had a very short life after that and the water fished like a bitch for about
three months thereafter. It was almost impossible to get a take on any bait, be it
boilie or particle.

I have read that tigers last almost indefinitely on the lake bed; that uneaten
bait will remain perfectly edible ages after it was introduced. This is not so. On
College they started to come up after about three weeks...and they smelt terrible!
No wonder the carp stopped having them.

To prepare tigers, you need to soak them for at least 24 hours, then boil them
for 20-30 minutes. You will find that the soaking period allows them to take on
water and swell up nicely, but you will never be able to cook them so that they
soften like other particles. After the bait has been cooked, return the tigers to a
bucket along with the water that they have been cooked in.

Again tigers are at their best as they start to ferment. After three or four days you will find the liquid in which they have been standing starts to thicken considerably, taking on the consistency of syrup. A handful of tigers, encompassed by the sticky liquid looks rather like frog spawn. The liquid smells slightly sour, but is in fact raw starch and sugar emitted by the nuts as they ferment.

The trouble with tigers is that they do the carp no nutritional good whatsoever. They pick them up, crunch them up in their throat teeth and pass them straight through their gut in about 20 minutes. Anyone who has sacked a carp that has been eating tigers will have seen the excreted particles of tiger nut in the bottom of the sack. Some nuts even pass through the system intact, and at best each nut is only broken into four or five sharp-edged pieces by the throat teeth. You can see just what a problem that may cause to the carp's digestive system and carp that have been on the tigers often display a raw anal vent.

In addition, tigers are a self perpetuating bait, especially if too much is introduced. Imagine that a number of anglers bait up with, say two or three kilos of tigers each for a weekend session. A couple may catch carp which leads to yet more going in. Results show an improvement the following weekend, so yet more tigers are introduced – more fish means more tigers. This may last three or four weekends, then suddenly the action slows and finally, goes dead.

This is what I believe might be happening.

The first time the tigers went in a few carp came in on the baited areas and started to eat the bait. They ate their fill and moved off, and twenty to thirty minutes later they all started excreting half eaten tuger nuts. The pieces of bait were all still perfectly edible and in all probability were picked up by other carp, or even eaten again by the same carp that had excreted them in the first place! So the tigers spread themselves all over the lake bed, with the aid of the carp's digestive system. As more bait was introduced, so more carp fed on the baited area and yet more half eaten bait was spread all over the lake bed after passing through one or sometimes two digestive systems. The bait was self-perpetuating and after a short period of time saturation point was reached. By now the carp were thoroughly fed up with tiger nuts and stopped eating both freshly introduced whole nuts and crunched up ones that had passed through their guts to be spread far and wide over the lake bed.

The result was sick carp with damaged guts, unable to feed properly and spooky as hell of tiger nuts. The lake starts to fish like a pudding until either the carp feel more inclined to feed, or all the stinking nuts have come up and the lake bed is refreshed.

Personally I don't use tigers and never will, but don't let me put you off them. If they are permitted on your water, they can be an excellent short term summer bait. The watchword with tiger nuts is, do not use too much, and you'll be surprised just how little can qualify as too much!

PEANUTS

Opinion is divided on the subject of peanuts as a carp bait. Sure, they catch carp, and certainly carp appear willing to eat vast amounts of the nuts, but in the early 80's the over-zealous use of peanuts was responsible for many carp deaths in heavily fished lakes. On College we lost some of our best fish following the widespread use of masses of peanuts. The fish lost condition and weight and some

Boilie soup showing its consistency.

Boilie soup/Cobra Groundbaiter Spoon.
Note the soup breaking up quickly as it hits the water.

died. The same applied on lakes in the Home Counties and the north.

In this country all peanuts are screened for a highly carcinogenic (cancer-producing) substance. Only those that pass the screening are allowed to go for human consumption. The ones that fail the screening are sold off as bird feeds. These nuts are often used as carp baits as they are considerably cheaper than nuts that have passed the screening test. There is every risk that these poor quality, carcinogenic peanuts can cause cancers in carp. Is that what you want?

Even peanuts that have been passed as fit for human consumption cause vitamin E deficiency in carp. Lack of vitamin E causes weight loss and in extreme cases, death. A fish can lose up to 30% of its body weight due to vitamin E deficiency and this weight loss may be impossible to regain. In addition carp generally lose condition as well as weight and this unhealthy state may stunt their full potential for their entire lifetime.

It follows therefore that if you are going to use peanuts, ALWAYS use nuts that are sold for human consumption.

(From a human point of view, NEVER eat nuts that are sold as bird foods – not unless you want cancer, that is!)

Having got the scare tactics out of the way, let me tell you how to use peanuts sensibly and with consideration. I would never use uncooked peanuts, though many anglers prefer them uncooked. I think that peanuts attract because of their high oil content and this cannot be released without cooking. I also like to flavour peanuts. To prepare the nuts simply soak them overnight and boil them for 15-20 minutes. Strain off the water and allow them to cool. This will produce a soft nut with an oil content that has been emulsified by the heat making it easier for it to seep out into the water.

Peanuts also exude a thick milky substance after two or three days and as with maples and tigers, this is when they are at their best.

Though carp seem quite prepared to eat a lot of peanuts, offering them a big carpet of bait is irresponsible. I prefer to use the extra-large South American peanuts. After preparation these swell to 12-14mm in size and I regard each nut as an individual bait. Ten or a dozen nuts catapulted widely around each hookbait is ample. Please bear in mind the health risks of excessive use of peanuts. Many fisheries impose a total ban on peanuts, and with good reason. If you must use them, do so with the utmost care and consideration.

BLACK-EYED BEANS

Along with maples, this is one of the best particles of all time. In the late 70's this was a bait that accounted for a huge number of carp from all over the UK. The definitive advice on all particles came from Rod Hutchinson. His articles in Angling magazine spelt out the way forward with these baits and black-eyes were one of Rod's favourites. I was firmly under the Hutchinson spell and tomato-flavoured beans were the ace up my sleeve on my home waters for a time. I also did exceptionally well with beans flavoured and coloured with turmeric, an Indian spice that turns black-eyes bright yellow.

Prepare as you would maples, allowing the cooked beans to stand for three or four days until they begin to smell slightly 'off'.

Black-eyed beans make an excellent particle bait that can be absolutely instant. It is another particle that carp seem prepared to eat a lot of, but they are also very filling so do not make the mistake of overbaiting. This will only lead to a temporary switch-off after the carp have gorged themselves on the beans. For sustained action bait up with just three or four pouches of bait around each hookbait.

SWEETCORN

Probably the first particle bait to be used, and certainly one of the best of all the particles. The previous record carp caught by Chris Yates in 1981 from Redmire Pool was tempted on sweetcorn and it was at Redmire that the particle was first used, in 1972. Sweetcorn accounted for some remarkable catches from Redmire during the 70s, the most successful angler being Kevin Clifford who caught fifteen twenties and a thirty on the bait in the summer of 1975. Kevin's results could not be kept quiet for long and soon sweetcorn was in widespread use all over the UK. Some of my earliest memories of Salamander Lake include float-fishing sweetcorn in the holes in the weed by the inlet. They went mad for it, but I found that they soon became very spooky of the little yellow grains. My experience was mirrored by many other anglers; it seemed sweetcorn was good for about three months and that was it.

Of course, the top carp men got their thinking caps on and started adding flavours and colour to sweetcorn and suddenly the bait took on a new lease of life. Nowadays tins of dyed and flavoured sweetcorn is widely available, and in France the giant Sensas company has recently launched an own-label range of tinned sweetcorn, containing that company's own range of flavours, sweeteners and colours.

Things have come full circle on Salamander. In 1997 many of the best fish to come out fell for flavoured sweetcorn once again.

So that's a look at some of the best particles. As I said at the beginning of this chapter, I believe that boilies catch bigger and better fish, and I also believe that you can achieve a better effect using pellets or ball pellets, but there is no escaping the fact that certain particles do catch carp. If you think they might give you an edge on the water you are fishing, then I strongly recommend that you use them, but please do bear in mind that they are unlikely to have a long catching life and if you use some particles to excess you may well be putting your carp at risk for the sake of short term satisfaction.

MINI-BOILIES AND CHOPPED BAITS

By far the best way to fish a particle strategy is with mini-boilies. Unfortunately apaart from the laborious chore of making them yourself, there is no easy way to prepare thousands of small, round baits other than to buy 6-8mm ready-made. However, if you are prepared to do the hard work and make tiny boiled baits or chopped mini'sausages', there is no better particle bait. If you add an equal amount of chopped or crushed boilies and soak the baits for 24-48 hours in neat flavour or amino acid liquid food, you will have prepared a bucket of bait that will fish the socks of any of the previously mentioned particle baits...and you'll do the carp some good into the bargain.

If I want to attract as many heavily feeding carp into my swim at one time, I plump for a liberal carpet of groundbait or pellets, topped off with an equal quan-

Mini-boilies and chopped baits; the BEST way to fish a particle strategy.

tity of mini-boilies and chopped and crushed baits. That approach is a sure-fire winner and it has worked for me whenever and wherever I have used it. I realise there is hard work involved, but if a job's worth doing...and all that!

20. A Summary of Baits and Ingredients

That brings us to the end of this in-depth look at carp baits. I hope all of you who have read this book will have gained something from it. Maybe not, "all you wanted to know, but were afraid to ask", but at least perhaps a nugget or two to help you put more carp on the bank. One thing I have to stress: there is no such thing as the ultimate carp bait. No matter how appetising and appealing a bait may be, there are times when they are just not having it. There's nothing you can do to make them have it, and as Ritchie McDonald once said, "There are times when you just have to sit and wait!"

Regardless of what you may think at times, when others seem to be catching more than their share, they are almost certainly using a bait that fulfils one or more of the criteria explained in this book. There are no magic ingredients! There is no wonder bait!

Let's close these pages with a final summary of ingredients and baits.

FISHMEALS

A fishmeal is a heat-dried, dehydrated powder made up from either whole fish or from the remains of the fish after it has been processed for human consumption. Many small fish such as anchovy, sand-eel, capelin and sardine are processed whole so that the resulting meal consists of the entire fish, including bones and offal.

Fishmeals are used in the pet food industry for making tinned pet foods, by the fish farming industry where they are used in the manufacture of fish pellets for commercially reared fish, and in agriculture, where they are used as fertilisers. Fishmeals are sold in various grades of quality and some of the industrial forms of fishmeal are not intended for consumption by living creatures and should be avoided. The best quality fishmeals are screened for bacteria, mould-inducing infections and for rancidity, as well as for oil and protein content, but it is still essential always to use the freshest products available.

Here are some of the most widely used fishmeals.

WHITE FISH MEAL – often sold under its trade name of PROVIMI 66. This is a dried powder that is made up from the ground bones and the remaining flesh after processing white fish such as cod, ling, hake and whiting for the frozen food market. It has a strong, distinctive smell and a protein value of 65%. It is quite a dense meal so it is useful as a bulking agent and for making heavy baits for long range fishing. Oil content is usually in the region of 8-12% and where possible I would recommend the meal with the lowest oil content for longer shelf life and better nutritional qualities.

CAPELIN MEAL is an expensive fish meal that comes mainly from Scandinavia and Iceland. It is processed from the whole fish, a close relative of the salmon, which is harvested by industrial trawlers that catch the tiny fish in huge quantities during a comparatively short season. It too has a very distinctive smell and colour and a high protein content of around 70%. The meal is widely used by the trout and salmon fish-farming industry to manufacture the best quality fish pellets. It is also used as a commercial food ingredient in pellets specially formulated for the rearing of farmed carp. It has been shown that carp are very partial to the taste, smell and digestibility of capelin meal, so it follows that any base mix incorporating a percentage of capelin meal will be more effective than one without the meal in it.

SARDINE MEAL AND ANCHOVY MEAL is a blend of two fishmeals that used to be available individually. Together they result in a very fine powder with an exceptionally high biological food value and for this reason it too is widely used to make feed pellets. Sardine and anchovy meal is probably the most popular of all the fishmeals with carp anglers and bait companies.

CODLIVINE is a vitamin and mineral feed supplement intended for horses. It is based on cod liver oil, processed white fish, molasses, bran and maize meal. Though not particularly high in protein, it is rich in essential vitamins and minerals and it also has a high fat content. It is rich in carbohydrates (mainly sugars) and is a well balanced total food. It is an excellent addition to any home made blend of fishmeals, but it is not used much by the bait companies due to its high cost.

FISH OILS are as important a factor in a fishmeal bait as the base mix itself. It has been widely accepted that excessive levels of fish oils (or any food oil for

Choosing the right ingredients helped tempt this fine 32 pounder (14.5kg) for Ken.

that matter) is very bad for the health of the carp and can even cause death. As there is a built-in oil content in all fishmeals anyway, it is highly irresponsible to include excessive levels of fish oil in a bait. Levels as high as 40ml/500g were common not so long ago but now the practice of adding such a level is frowned upon. Many UK fisheries now impose a limit on the amount of fish oil that can be used in boiled baits on their lakes, usually no more than 10ml/500g. However, don't think that because they can cause health problems when used to excess, they are totally bad for carp. Fish oils provide a long-term fat source which can be converted into energy, thus allowing the carp to use the protein content of your bait for the important job of promoting growth and general health. In addition fish oils can be used as attractors in their own right as they spread their unique attraction over a wide area once sufficient free samples have been introduced to the lake.

There is an obvious adverse reaction between fish oils and lake water in that they don't mix together. As water permeates the bait, oil is driven out in the form of tiny droplets which float to the surface. With a lot of baits in the water the resulting spread of attraction can cover a considerable area and any fish that swims through that area, be it at the surface, near to the bottom or anywhere in between will sense the presence of the stimulatory oil and be encouraged to investigate this enticing smell of food. The track leads them straight down to your baits!

Some fish oils are more dense than others and salmon oil, for instance, will form tiny droplets close to the lake bed, rather than at the surface. Popular fish oils include, sardine oil, mackerel oil, cod liver oil, pilchard oil and, to my mind the most effective, pure salmon oil. Most fish oils are likely to become considerably thicker and much less effective during colder weather, and though this can affect the way that the oil disperses from the bait, it does not detract from the oil's overall nutritional qualities. Some fish oils are now treated to prevent thickening. These are known as 'winterised' oils. For instance, winterised pilchard oil is very effective once the water temperatures start to fall as winter sets in. Not all oils are prone to thickening; salmon oil is one that isn't.

There is another inherent problem with fish oils, that of rancidity which causes the oil to deteriorate and become indigestible and hazardous to the fish's health. Most reputable bait firms now add some form of anti-oxidant to their products in order to prevent rancidity.

BIRDFOODS

Birdfoods have several advantages over alternative ingredients in that they are cheap, highly digestible and are often fairly instant with no need for a pre-baiting programme to wean the carp onto them. That said, it is my experience of such baits that they only reach their true potential once a lot of bait has been introduced, or there is a bait team on the water, all using the same birdfood base mix and flavours.

As their name suggests, many of the best ingredients have been designed as supplementary feeds for show birds and racing pigeons. They contain a mixture of seeds, biscuit meal and bran, the most popular seeds being ground or crushed hemp, crushed maize, rape and dari seeds, and in some cases linseed or even poppy seed. Birdfoods are not usually high in protein, but they always contain a high level of fats. As with fishmeal baits, birdfood baits provide the carp with energy, which in turn allows the protein content to be used for growth and tissue repair.

Birdfoods are mostly coarse textured and are particularly popular in winter when the gritty nature of the finished boiled bait allows a better leak-off of flavours, sweeteners and other liquid attractors.

Here are some of the most popular birdfood ingredients.

ROBIN RED CONCENTRATE is the famous ingredient renowned for turning your hands, bowls, wooden spoons and everything else in the kitchen a dark red colour, and an important and logical starting point for many carp bait recipes. Designed as a feed for show birds to enhance the red colours in their plumage, this dark, highly concentrated red ingredient is far more than just a dye. Undoubtedly its prime attraction lies in the inclusion of the synthetic vitamin, Carophyll Red which, it seems, carp find practically irresistible. The product also contains other significant natural products such as paprika and red pepper, and Robin Red can be improved still further by the addition of a small amount of ground black pepper and ground dried onion. Star Baits, distributed by Sensas, offer their own base mix called Robin Red Bird Food as well as other assorted birdfood bases.

RED FACTOR is another birdfood containing Carophyll Red, and one that is almost as good as Robin Red. It is used extensively by bait companies, often at high concentrations of up to 50% of total dry weight. A simple yet effective recipe comprises just two ingredients, Red Factor and semolina mixed in equal quantities.

RED BAND is a blend of seeds intended as a canary feed. It needs to be ground to a coarse powder in a coffee grinder before it can be used but it is a fantastic bait ingredient. Like many canary feeds the seed blend in Red Factor is high in natural binders and by simply adding boiling water the glutinous, sticky residue thus formed is instantly attractive to carp. It also contains a small amount of Carophyll Red.

P.T.X. is a dark, sweet, molasses-based meal that is often used in combination with sweet flavours rather than fruity or savoury ones. Certainly the sweetness of the original product comes out in the taste of the bait, and when used with low levels of caramel, toffee or cream flavours, P.T.X. really comes into its own.

PROSECTO INSECTIVEROUS is a similar product to P.T.X. but it is not as sweet. Believe it or not, it contains crushed dried insects – there's protein for you! Because of their sticky base of molasses and honey, both PTX and Prosecto have relatively short shelf lives. It is best to buy in small quantities to ensure freshness.

NECTABLEND was one of the first bulk birdfood ingredients to be used and it is now widely used in many base mixes. It is a bright yellow mid-protein blend of egg biscuit and seeds, including a small proportion of niger seed, which carp seem to adore. I have found that it works better when crushed or ground to a fine powder, but most bait firms that use Nectablend in their mixes use it in its coarse original form. As such it allows a superb leak-off of liquid flavours, attractors and oils. Proprietary mixes such as Solar's Yellow Seed Mix and Nutrabaits' Enervite Gold contain a high proportion of Nectablend.

All the above ingredients come from J.E.Haith of Cleethorpes. Their telephone number is: 01472-357515. You owe it to yourself to give them a ring!

SLUIS C.L.O. is a seed based birdfood with a fabulous pedigree. It is a complete natural food in its own right but by coincidence is also an excellent binder, one that is often used in birdfood bases as well as in many fishmeal mixes. C.L.O. has an added, highly attractive food oil which a vital part of its nutritional attraction.

In addition to the basic ingredients mentioned above, most bait companies add their own secret ingredients which they hope will give their products an edge. For instance, Enervite contains Liver Powder and Dried Brewers Yeast, both renowned carp attractors, while Solar's Savay Seed Mix contains its own distinctive sweet attractor and taste enhancer.

VITAMEALO is a calf milk powder which is used for weaning young calves onto their mothers milk. It is heavily sweetened and flavoured with cream or vanilla attractors which we know are very attractive to carp. It has a very high fat content which supplements the natural fats already present in birdfoods, and has a very distinctive taste and smell. You can add 15-20% of Vitamealo to any base mixes in order to provide a more acceptable sweet, vanilla smell and taste. It is ideal for use in birdfood mixes as many of these are bland and tasteless on their own.

HIGH PROTEIN HNV BAITS

Milk, whey, soya and egg protein baits have been around even longer than fish-meals and birdfood baits. Way back at the very beginning of what we could term modern carp fishing, Fred Wilton's original casein-based bait created headlines on carp lakes all over the country. Since then they have come and gone to varying degrees, but high protein HNV baits are never far from the lips of the participants in any bait discussion. Many thought that they had died a death by the end of the seventies, but when Rod Hutchinson came along with his own very distinctive bait as described in "The Carp Strikes Back" and his success on the very diffi-cult Savay Lake revived the whole issue all over again.

Let's have a close look at some of the ingredients that are most often used in such HNV baits.

CASEIN. There are two types of edible, food grade casein. Acid casein and Rennet Casein. I won't go into the details of how they differ apart from telling you that they have different pH values, which may or may not be of interest to you.

Rennet casein is my own favourite and I use it to make up 50% of any protein mix. In combination with other binding ingredients and with a boiling time of less than 50 seconds, I can achieve a hard outer shelled bait with a paste centre.

Acid casein is available in two types, 30 mesh and 100 mesh. The coarser version is used to obtain a hard-centred bait, while 100 mesh casein is much finer and is a useful alternative to rennet casein in a soft-centred bait. I would not suggest you use more than 30% of either acid caseins in a mix. The bait firms that still include a genuine milk and egg protein HNV in their product list usually blend a mix of all three caseins in order to achieve a perfect balance of protein, vitamins and minerals. Some of the best caseins come from Holland and from France, though for a while the superb rennet casein produced by Express Food Industries was the best money could buy. Sadly this fabulous product is no longer made in the UK.

CALCIUM CASEINATE. This is a fine, very light milk protein. Its main attraction is its water solubility, allowing a better leak-off of the stimulatory mes-sages from milk products that are known to be significantly attractive to carp.

SODIUM CASEINATE is a stickier, lighter, water-soluble protein extracted from acid casein. In the hay-day of paste baits the product was used as a protein ingredient and as a binder. It is notoriously sticky to work with, and I would include it only as a small part of an overall package in order to improve a better protein balance. Its main advantage is that it is extremely light, so it can be used to make slow sinking, semi-buoyant baits.

LACTALBUMIN is another milk protein that was once widely used in HNV baits. Lately however, it has become less popular since the limitations of its poor shelf life were fully realised. Stabilised lactalbumin-like products such as Nutralac are now a much more convienient and more suitable product.

EGG ALBUMIN is the isolated protein of the white of egg. It is used in the ice-cream and cake industries and only this top grade of the product is used by the reputable bait firms. Animal grade egg albumin is less refined and not as stable. Its prime use in HNV baits is to cut down on the amount of boiling time needed to achieve a hard outer skin on a bait. The longer milk proteins are boiled, the more they coagulate and the more the protein is destroyed. By using egg albumin, the boiling time can be kept to a minimum, thus protecting the sensitive proteins from the effects of excessive heat. An interesting side effect of egg albumin is its ability to act as an almost instant binder and boilie toughener, though it should be stressed that it is also a highly nutritious and digestible ingredient. If you are encountering problems whereby your baits are breaking up in flight after leaving a throwing stick, the addition of 50g of egg albumin to your base mix will harden the bait significantly and should stop the problem recurring.

WHEY PROTEIN is used to give a better overall protein profile. It is added to milk, soya and egg proteins so as to provide the few amino acids that are not present in those proteins. It is also a binder and it has a smooth, slightly sweet taste that adds considerably to any base mix. An example of a whey protein is NUTRAPRO from the Rotherham-based company Nutrabaits.

LIQUID FOOD ADDITIVES while not, in fact, a solid food ingredient are very useful and important additions to any base mix. This is because they are actually pure foodstuffs in a bottle! You can add them at just about any level you can afford – the whole bottle if you are rich enough – in order to increase the nutritional value of your bait, at the same time making them more attractive to carp due to their high concentrations of amino acids, vitamins and minerals. They are superb attractors as they release 'free' aminos into the lake water around each individual boilie, thus drawing carp from far and wide to investigate their enticing food smell. They also have a taste profile that carp simply adore – truly one of the best types of bait additive imaginable.

Some of the best liquid foods include the Sense Appeal range, Starmino, Amino Blend Supreme, Minamino, Nutramino, Multimino-PPC and Corn Steep Liquor. All these liquids act as a feed supplement and can turn even a relatively low protein bait into a very effective food bait as 50ml of Nutramino or Minamino is the equivalent of 75g of pure pre-digested protein.

Now let's look at some of the more popular bulking ingredients.

SEMOLINA is widely used in the bait industry to bind and complement other ingredients. It is of limited food value, but it is high in carbohydrates which are an important part of a carp's diet. There is no getting away from the fact that carp like the taste of semolina and countless thousands of fish have fallen to semolina-based baits of a relatively low food value. It helps the bait roll into sausage shapes and will boil right through the bait to make a rock-hard boilie; very useful when your lake is teeming with crayfish or poisson-chat.

FULL FAT SOYA FLOUR is another bulking ingredient used to enhance the

fat and protein profile of a base mix. I have my reservations about all soya products because there is evidence that soya is an inhibitor of the protein digesting
enzyme, trypsin, which is the carp's primary enzyme within its gut. Mind you, I
have to say that loads of carp are caught on soya/semo baits and it doesn't seem to
be doing them any harm. After all, most ready-made boilies on sale in your local
tackle shop are made up of basically only two ingredients, semolina and soya flour,
and you don't need me to tell you how effective ready-mades are.

MAIZE MEAL is simply fine ground maize. It is used to make cattle feeds,
trout pellets and a whole host of feed pellets and foodstuffs for animals and birds.
It has a high protein content and because of this and its overall better nutritional
importance, Maize Meal is in my opinion a far better bulk ingredient than either
semolina or soya flour.

KELP POWDER is a brilliantly effective, highly nutritious product rich in
trace elements such as Vitamin E. It is known that carp find it highly stimulatory
to both their smell and their taste organs. Because of its cost it is generally used
very sparingly at around 25-30g per 500g of base mix, but because I can obtain
seaweed products in bulk and at trade prices I have used both kelp and seaweed
products to make up as much as 50% of the total dry weight, and very effective it
was too!

DRIED SEAWEED is a coarse product which ends up as tiny particles within
the bait. The product is high in valuable trace elements, amino acids and vitamins.
It is generally available at horse chandlers or riding stables as it is used as a con-
ditioner for race and show horses. It has a very distinctive texture and smell and
will create a very 'different' boilie. It can be used at up to 100g/kg.

GREEN LIPPED MUSSEL EXTRACT is one of the most effective attractors
yet discovered. It is a highly concentrated powdered extract, originating from a
shellfish found in the warm Pacific waters off New Zealand. The product is high
in betaine, a natural chemical that is known to be attractive to carp. More importantly, betaine has been known to incite an active and sustained feeding response
when used at exactly the right level in combination with certain amino acids.
Unfortunately this "exactly right" level and the amino acid combination is a
closely guarded secret known only to the fish farming industry and lesser mortals
like carp anglers are not apparently privvy to the secret!

Green lipped mussel extract also has a very strong shellfish smell and taste.
It is expensive which tends to limit its level of use within a base mix, but to be
honest I have not yet found an upper limit of inclusion of this product. In other
words you can't put enough of the stuff into your base mix! So, the richer you are
the more you can afford to use! However, I suggest you try no more than 2g/500g
dry mix.

LIVER POWDER has been around for many years and many of the top bait
gurus have advocated its use for some time now. Certainly the track record of powdered liver speaks for itself, as carp find the product highly attractive due to the
balanced spread of amino acids, vitamins and minerals therein. You can use as
much or as little as you wish within a bait, depending on how rich you are! I would
suggest no more than 5g/500g and in fact I have had excellent results at as little as
1g/500g.

SHRIMP EXTRACT is a totally natural extract that is tailor-made for inclusion within fishmeal baits. Most of the best shrimp meals and extracts originate in
Denmark. Again the inclusion levels are a matter for individual tastes but person-

ally I would not suggest using more than 2g/500g as there is evidence to suggest that higher levels could lead to your baits becoming too bouyant and they may float.

BETAINE HYDROCHLORIDE is simply the best carp attractor of all time. It is, if you like, the natural smell of food that carp find in their everyday existence. It is present in many forms of natural food such as crustacea, worms, nymphs and bloodworms as well as being present in plants, fungi, the flesh of fish and molluscs. It has long been recognised as a primary feeding stimulant by fish farmers who include it in many feed pellets and commercial feeds. It can be used to great effect in any type of base mix, and because of its super-soluble nature it can be dissolved in flavours, liquid foods and in water for use as an external soak or bait spray. It is without doubt the most effective bait additive yet discovered and its track record for putting fish on the bank is second to none. I would sooner go out without my trousers on than fish a carp bait that does not contain Betaine HCl!

Thank you for reading this book; now get out there and DO IT!

21. Bait Companies
Guest Chapter

(Please note, the opinions expressed herein are those of the proprietors of individual bait companies and are not necessarily those of the author.)

KEVIN MADDOCKS OF KM CARP BAITS

In my 25 years or so of carp fishing I have always believed that the taste of our baits is far more important than the smell. It is because I feel so strongly about this that I am amazed every time I meet a carp angler who doesn't taste his baits. It is a fact beyond doubt that thousands of carp fishers never taste their baits and I know from my own experience that if they did they would catch more fish.

The first time I ever saw a boilie, in the early 70's, I ate it! I needed to know what it tasted like and I have eaten all my baits ever since, and anyone else's that I could get my teeth into. I have also eaten (not just tasted) all of the carp's natural food – shrimp, mussels, bloodworm and other small invertebrae. By doing this I have tasted many foods and baits that the carp like and many that they don't like. I believe that this experience inevitably helps me catch more fish; I can taste a bait without field testing it and have a good idea if it is going to be a good catcher or not.

Over the years I have strived to use baits that were quite strong in smell but with a low taste. In the early days, before I used liquid flavours, this was relatively easy to achieve. Our natural squid and octopus boilies, and our pilchard flavoured Munchies boilies, just to name two, were high in smell and low in taste. These two baits, plus others that contained no liquid flavours, were some of the most successful boilies ever. We slaughtered the fish on every lake we fished, getting far more takes that anyone else. This was pre-hair rig days and I strongly believe that it was (and still is, somewhat, today) due to the taste of the baits. Virtually everyone else's bait that I tasted were at least twice as strong as ours and many had a bitter after-taste caused by the liquid flavour.

Whilst I will always readily confess that I am no expert on bait, I have certainly proved to myself that carp recognise the 'carrier' on which a flavour is based. In my opinion the flavour's carrier or base is quite often more important than the flavour itself or the ingredients. You can prove this to yourself by catching well on a lake with a particular flavour, say tangerine on a monoproplyene glycol (P.G.) base and then when the catches have tailed off, replace it with a different flavour, say Indian Spice, but on the same base. Usually the catches will only slightly improve...but then change the Indian Spice to a completely different base and catches will greatly improve. (Always remember that this is providing everything is equal, which is often not the case in carp fishing. You might change to that Indian Spice and not succeed simply because someone else has just 'hammered' the water on your 'new' base!) This proves that the flavour's base can be of paramount importance.

The bases on which the majority of today's flavours are based such as P.G., I.P.A., etc taste somewhat harsh. The carp don't like this and if you taste this harshness yourself (in diluted form, remember), you will certainly agree with the carp: they are evil! The harshness of these types of flavours is partially because the bases are water soluble. Thus mixing immediately with water (or saliva in our case) releases all the aromatics in one go. This harshness is also accentuated by the fact that the bases taste somewhat harsh on their own.

In recent years I have experimented with different carriers and in 1995 I came up with a particular, rarely used, natural oil. This was highly refined, had no noticeable taste or smell, was unaffected by cold water, and was very expensive! We employed a highly skilled flavourist to blend a natural strawberry oil with this 'new' carrier, plus one or two other minor goodies. We named it Strawberry SR35 and it scored very heavily on the waters we used it on; you only need to ask anyone who used it! We continued experimenting and soon found that we could increase the smell without any really noticeable change to the taste. Oils have a quenching effect on the taste because they tend to hold back the flavour components, preventing them from dissolving all at once. I was at last producing a flavour which fulfilled my long held belief that a relatively high smell but low taste is far superior.

A year later our flavourist, one of the best in the country, had blended a very

This is when getting the correct levels of smell/taste is paramount – Kevin with an immaculate common of 30.5 pounds (13.9kg) taken in mid-winter.

special range of nine smells for us on the unique base. Each one was quietly field tested as much as possible and with another year further on we have been able to launch what I believe to be one of the best ranges available. Most, if not all, of the flavours used for carp fishing are simply mass-produced food grade flavours re-packaged. I can proudly say that our new Liquid Smells have been produced solely for carp fishing and you will not find anything quite like them in today's food or bait industries. If you are looking for a new flavour, why not give them a try? One thing is for certain, the chances are that no-one else has used them yet on your lake. They are available in: Strawberry, Peach, Rosehip, Squid, Indian Spice, Tangerine, Prawn & Shrimp, Double Cream, and Monster Mussel. If you have difficulty finding a stockist, you can order them through any decent tackle shop – most have an account with the distributors, Beekay International – and can simply telephone the order through for you. If you encounter difficulies, please report this directly to Beekay (details elsewhere in this book) who will willingly sort out the problem for you.

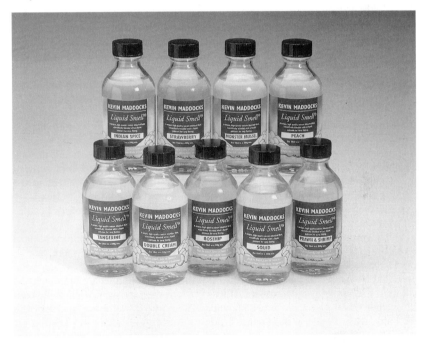

The KM Liquid Smells – a totally new concept in carp attraction.

ALAN TAYLOR OF WHACKER CATCHER PRODUCTS

Just how good is the Withy Pool mix, you might ask? Well, to help you make your mind up I should like to tell you the story of last summer's fishing.

Richard Billington, Martin Walker and myself used the mix at Kevin Maddocks' Withy Pool. The draw for swims was made, then two weeks prior to the start of the season we decided we would start to introduce the bait. There were to be eleven anglers fishing at the start with several bait teams involved. Like most of the fishing at Withy Pool it would be close-in fishing; baiting up easy from the bank and better still, by climbing the trees and crawling into the bankside bushes we could see if our bait was being eaten and observe the carp's reactions to the bait. Due to our success the previous season with the mix, our hopes were, of course, very high.

I started introducing the bait in small quantities to all the known feeding spots and anywhere else that I saw carp. There are twenty big carp in Withy and most of the time a few can be found tucked away under the trees in the snags or held up in the weed. After my first couple of visits I only put bait into the swims I knew that we would be fishing. On my third visit of baiting I was caught unawares and as I walked into The Double, Richard's swim, a large carp bow waved out. I quietly crept into the bush to the right of the swim and saw two big carp circling in and out of the snags. As they moved out five yards or so from the snag I dropped in a handful of baits. Sure enough, after a couple of minutes one returned and as the carp got within a yard of the baits, it froze. It stopped instantly, as if it had seen something it was scared of, its fins remained rigid and it did not move for a minute or so until gradually its pectoral fins began fanning the water, its gills started pumping and it gradually approached the bait. It slowly tipped up in the water as it approached the first bait and took it without any hesitation. I expected it to suck and blow, or at least take its time, but no, it took the first one and kept its head down until all the baits had gone. It then continued to really root about in the bottom looking for more bait. While it was doing this, another big carp joined in. I sat mesmerised until they had finished. I quickly baited the other spots as I couldn't wait to tell Richard and Martin.

The next time I went to bait up was a Saturday so I had plenty of time to have a really good look around. The spots where we had been baiting were getting clearer and clearer and the weed was almost non-existent where it had been uprooted by the feeding carp. They had polished the bottom clean, removing the silt until the hard clay was exposed. It was obvious the carp were well on the bait.

On my next visit I saw a fish known as The Forty. It was about one foot from the bank, tucked under a huge snag. I didn't want to spook it but was keen to get baited up and away so I decided to put the bait in singularly instead of the usual handfuls. As the second bait hit the water the carp moved off. I thought it had been spooked but as it shot forward it grabbed a bait that was falling though the water in front of it. The fish seemed quite happy though it did spook him a bit and he slowly moved out of the swim. I quickly put in the rest of the bait in time for it to return along with three others. I watched as they devoured the baits, then they churned up the bottom looking for more, or so I thought. In fact they were feeding so frantically and taking more than one bait in at a time that as they crushed the baits particles were being blown out through their gills, which left little particles of bait littered about the swim. The carp could obviously still smell these and were hunting for every last bit. I could not wait to tell Martin and Richard. We were all

Terry Eustace
Gold Label Tackle

Many lines now claim to have abrasion resistance - what does that mean? It means having the potential to resist being damaged by contact with weed, snags, branches, rocks and gravel bars.

We have tested Pro-Gold against other leading lines which claim to have abrasion resistance. Using 12lb line in tests, pulling our competitors' lines over an abrasive edge (using the same weight for each test) they all broke after 2 to 15 lifts of the weight.

We conducted hundreds and hundreds of tests. One line recognised as the 'toughest line available' (we only had this in 14lb test) consistently broke after 11 or 12 lifts. One line making all sorts of abrasion resistance claims consistently broke at between 1 and 3 lifts of the weight. We stopped the Pro-Gold tests after 100 lifts when

we had proved our point and the person watching had got bored! When tested to destruction, Pro-Gold notched up an impressive 180 cycles.

So what is the main factor which causes us to lose fish? Apart from bad knots it has to be abrasion. Even the most insignificant branch can do untold damage to your line when dragged around it speedily by a fast running fish. Your line meets up with all sorts of unseen, unsuspected obstacles when you are playing the fish. It simply wouldn't break otherwise.

YOU must choose a soft line for distance casting, delicate presentation when floater fishing, accuracy when casting to precise marks and for trouble free (doesn't spring off the spool like wire) reel loading.

YOU must choose a line which will withstand abrasion caused by branches, tin cans, bars, mussels, tough weeds and the odd length of barbed wire.

YOU can now buy a line which will satisfy all these requirements.
Pro-Gold. Strictly Specimen.

Pro Gold
STRICTLY SPECIMEN
Terry Eustace
Gold Label Tackle

- Advanced Co-Polymer Technology
- Up to 20 times more abrasion resistant than other leading monos
- Extra Supple with low memory
- Designed for use with fixed spool reels
- Low Visibility Weed Green Colour
- Precise diameters

12lb TEST
1000 YARD SPOOL
(900 metres)
AVERAGE DIA .014" .355mm

LINE	SANDPAPER ABRASION CYCLES TO BREAK
TOP SELLING 12LB GERMAN MONO	7
12LB CARP LINE CLAIMING EXTRA ABRASION RESISTANCE	2
TOP SELLING 12LB ABRASION RESISTANT AMERICAN MONO	9
AN EXTRA TOUGH 14LB ABRASION RESISTANT AMERICAN MONO	12
PRO-GOLD	100*

* AFTER 100 CYCLES PRO-GOLD STILL DID NOT BREAK

378 Boldmere Road, Boldmere, Sutton Coldfield B73 5EZ.
Tel: 0121 373 4523 Fax: 0121 377 7785

Nutrabaits' Cranberry Ball Pellets – before.

The Ball Pellets after dissolving.

Hinders boss, Bryan Jarrett, with a fabulous upper '20' caught on
boilie over Particle/'A' Mix.

Stuart Mead with one of the several 40 pounders (18.2kg) caught whilst
field-testing one of the KM Liquid Smells (Strawberry).

Kevin Maddocks regularly proves that his ready-mades are one of the most successful on the market – seen here with a 55 pounder (25kg) from France.

Whacker Catcher Products proprietor, Alan Taylor, with an amazing 40.5 pounder (18.4kg) – one of countless fish taken on The Withy Pool Mix.

really excited and couldn't wait for the off. We decided we would not put any bait in for a couple of days before the start of the season, hoping that the carp would then be searching for our bait. We knew that the crayfish, at certain times, could be a serious problem so we had air-dried our hookbaits in our special drying out bags (see Withy Pool video). These included normal sinking bottom baits, critically balanced ones, and pop-ups.

At last the start of the season arrived and I set up quite early to give myself a chance to put up the 'house' in plenty of time. I did this as slowly and as quietly as possible. I was able to keep casting and plumbing to an absolute minimum as I had already done this during the close season. I had marked my lines so a marker was not required. It was a simple matter of pulling off enough line and clipping it onto the spool just behind the marks. Three underarm casts and "Bingo!" the baits would all be perfectly positioned and the traps set.

We had been fishing about two hours before the first buzzer of the season was heard. I waited and prayed for a call. Sure enough! It was Richard! I dashed along in the dark to his swim and crouched down with net and torch. Over the net it came and the "Whacker Catcher" cry went out for the first time. The fish was weighed – it was 'Cluster' at its best weight of 34lb 12oz. We sacked it in deep water ready for the photos in the morning. There was no other action to anyone in the night. I had all my baits in shallow water and when the dawn broke and the day looked like being a scorcher, I rubbed my hands in anticipation. Sure enough, I was next. Mid-morning I knocked out the 'Fully Scaled Mirror'. It didn't make too much of a disturbance and apart from a host of people gathering in my swim, I felt quite confident of another. A good thing about having the marks on the line is that re-casting is simple – no need for markers, etc and generally you are on the exact spot first cast. Two-Nil to the Whacker Catcher crew and we were letting them know about it!

Richard Billington with one of his many huge carp caught on The Withy Pool Mix.

I re-baited the spot heavily where I had caught the 'Fully Scaled Mirror' as the fish were obviously having it. I climbed the big tree in the corner which gave me a great vantage point to overlook my swim. I sat up the tree for about an hour before I noticed a carp making its way down the tree line towards my baited area. I had just managed to scramble down the tree as my rod bleeped. As I looked down I noticed the line lift again and pull tight to the clip so I lifted the rod from the rests and pulled into the fish. The first couple of seconds were important because if I let it get its head down it would surely power off into the snags. The water level was quite low due to the previous year's hot summer, which meant less water in the snags, which in turn meant that the carp were more likely to head out into open water. Again after a short scrap into the net it tumbled, 'Son of Popeye'. Around the lake for the photos and as we were reminding the others it was 3-0 and they had no chance, I was completely dowsed with a bucket of water. In the afternoon Richard caught a ghost carp of 20lb and the 'Original Half-Linear' at 30lb 12oz.

The Whacker Catcher himself; Alan Taylor with a fabulous mid-30 (16kg).

5-0! Were we having it off or not? We were hoping that Martin would get off the mark soon as the carp were feeding, big style.

Martin's swim was not particularly good as any carp wanting to get to his baits had to cross many other angler's lines. Martin was fishing 'locked up' as he was fishing right on the edge of some big snags. That night Martin had a single bleep and as he looked up, his rod disappeared over the top of his buzzer!

"I don't believe it!" he screamed.

Well, that was amazing, but the next part was even more so. He quickly wound in one of his other rods to cast out to try and locate the missing rod. On his first cast he caught something and as he retrieved, slowly the tip of his rod gradually emerged from the water. Amazingly the hook on the spare rod had caught the tip ring of the missing one. He grabbed the rod, only to find the fish still attached. It was a catfish of 23lb. A few hours later Martin landed 'Gary Linear' at 29lb 12oz. I think we mentioned to the others fishing nearby about how the carp had to

Tracey Wilkins samples yet another '30' that couldn't resist The Withy Pool Mix.

swim in and out of their lines to get to Matin's, but at 6-0 we were buzzing. Some of the fish in Withy, like any other lake, are harder to catch – or get caught – than others. 'Gary Linear' was one such carp.

The next fish Richard caught was 'The Common' at 29lb 14oz and my next one was 'Fenners', an even more irregular visitor. At 8-0 we thought we had better call it a day – we could not understand why so many people wanted to help us pack up and get our gear out of our swims!

We carried on using the bait throughout the season and it was almost as if some of the fish had switched over to that bait solely. We were getting repeat captures of some of the fish and they were not being caught by anyone else. Richard caught the lake record at 44lb 4oz. I caught 'KM's Thirty-Five' at 40lb 12oz and it's still catching. I fished there with my girlfriend Tracey three times, now that it is day-ticket and we never blanked. Tracey landed 'Popeye's Mate' at 32lb 8oz, 'Lumpy Tail' at 31lb 8oz, 'Joey' at 35lb 10oz and 'Cluster' at 35lb. But that's another story.

The Withy Pool Mix has probably caught more carp than any other bait in the history of the Pool and it is still catching to this day, despite other top anglers using good baits. We know it will work on all waters, particularly for those who are the first to use it. Why don't you give it a try before someone else does!

Here is the recipe:
3ml WC Peach and Pepper Flavour
30ml Whacker Catcher Oil
30ml WC Powdered Cream (30ml in volumn)
5ml WC Betaine
6 eggs (size 2)
Add Withy Pool Mix until required conistency is achieved.

The road to success – all you need to complete the incredibly successful mix!

DAVE POXON OF ESSEX BAIT SERVICES

At Essex Bait Services we pride ourselves on service and quality of product. We are now in our 9th season. For the first six years we rolled bait for numerous anglers in and around Essex before expanding to a Nationwide mail order business in 1996. The response since then has been unbelieveable, so much so that we have had to move premises three times. We have now acquired a free range chicken farm which has enabled us to not only have our own free range eggs, but also to build as and when required, such as our new 2,000 square feet air drying unit for the new season. We have also invested £45,000 in new machinery. All our employees are experienced carp anglers and bait makers, so if you need any help, whether it is flavour levels, suggested recipes or advice, there is always someone on hand for an unbiased opinion.

As we are stockists of all major bait company's products you will always get worthwhile advice, not just a sales pitch. These companies include Nutrabaits, Solar, Nash, Premier, Mainline, D.T., and Intertceptor. As you can see, the range of companies is extensive, all being suppliers of only the highest quality products. This also means that you can mix and match various company's products to customise your own mix without going to several outlets. We roll all size baits from 10mm to 25mm and all orders are sent out fresh, not frozen, unless you state oth-

Essex Bait Services boss, Dave Poxon, with a good fish from Manor Farm.

erwise (such as air-dried), by a national carrier on a guaranteed 24-hour delivery.

Recently we have released the Nutrabaits Big Fix Mix Pellet. This pellet is a major step forward due to the fact that it is the first pellet made from a specific base mix rather than substituted ingredients. The bonus of this is that, for the first time, you actually have a pellet that matches your boilie in every way. They are available in 11mm and 16mm sizes and they breakdown to a complete bed of base mix within two to four hours, releasing all the in-built attractors of the base mix, causing a feeding frenzy among the carp. They tend to be very effective when fished together with Big Fish Mix boilies scattered lightly around the lake.

We have also arranged to manufacture and distrubute several bait products under the Leslies of Luton Insight label. In the range are a new birdseed mix pellet, a fishmeal pellet, a range of salmon and trout pastes and a range of specialist HNV pastes. These have been tested over the past eighteen months with excellent results. The salmon and trout pastes proved to be exceptionally successful on waters where trout pellets work well.

The Interceptor range of baits have gone through extensive field tests over a two year period by ten anglers on a wide variety of waters around the country. The Interceptor range includes the Fish Mix; the most successful of all the baits tested. This mix, like all the other mixes in the range, continued to catch successfully throughout the years of field tests. Ingredients include Robin Red, krill, Betaine, fishmeals and two milk proteins.

Interceptor Seed Mix, also very successul on all waters, works straight from the off. Ingredients include Red Factor, kelp, birdseeds, Betaine and milk proteins.

Interceptor Winter Mix is a very instant bait. The first time our field tester Jason Callaghan used the bait he caught three thirties and five twenties from Wintons in a three night session. On the next session he broke the lake record with a 40lb 10oz mirror and added a thirty and three twenties to this capture. Ingredients include seaweed, milk proteins, birdseeds and Betaine.

All the Interceptor range will be supplied for you ready-rolled for you to freeze. They come in sizes 10mm, 14mm, 18mm, 20mm and 25mm.

Next is a range of shelf life baits called the Intercontinental Euro Range. These are aimed at the angler fishing abroad, but they are all proven catchers that will work equally well in this country. They have a very high attraction level with a good, hard texture and include extras such as kelp, Betaine and powdered palatants. The range includes Condensed Milk (cream coloured), Dragon's Breath (yellow with a hot spicy curry flavour), Sweet Red Devils (sweet strawberry flavour), Rotten Squid (orange with stinking squid extract), Tropical Heat (orange, a blend of six fruit flavours) and a Salmon and Trout Paste Boilie.

Last in the range are the Interceptor Pellets of which there are two types. Firstly the Interceptor Fish Mix pellets with S + P Carp Attractors; same concept as the Big Fish Mix pellets but on the Interceptor base mix. Then there are the Super Salmon pellets. These have a high oil content and are produced using top quality salmon rearing products. They have a very slow breakdown rate of up to 24 hours so they can be used as hookbaits as well as free offerings. These pellets are totally different and are definitely the next step on from trout pellets. Available in size 14mm only.

May I wish you all the best in your carp fishing in the future. For any further information or advice, don't hesitate to phone. (Full details appear elsewhere in this book).

BRYAN JARRETT OF HINDERS OF SWINDON

Whether we realise it or not, each time an angler introduces any bait to a water he will be trying to fool the fish into accepting it. Let's take a reasonably stocked, moderate water and have a look at how we approach it. A high percentage of anglers will fire out 20-30 boilies...and hope! This method will work, but let's go one stage further. If we introduce say, a bed of particles into our swim and then a few boilies we have a situation where our chances are increased. Why? Because a particle is generally a food source that a carp is not frightened of eating. The carp's attention is held by the bed of particles and it becomes absorbed in the process of picking up small food items that are close in size to the natural food items eaten every day.

This instills confidence, they eat more voraciously and as a consequence are more likely to make a mistake and pick up your hookbait. After all, a boilie is only a manufactured particle, so the progressive step is to use the real thing. So let's go one stage further again. What if we fish a particle over a bed of particles? We are now getting much closer to creating a natural feeding environment. A carpet of particles will gently release natural oils, sugars and flavours into your swim

Boilie over Hinders Particle/Trout Pellets accounted for this lovely upper '20' for Bryan Jarrett.

against the option of a synthetically flavoured boilie. With Hinders Mega Hemp, its very size and texture is charactaristic of the common water snail, one of the carp's favourite natural foods. No wonder this can encourage a swim simmering with feeding fish.

Particles come in many shapes and sizes and there will definitely be one to suit every angling situation. Here are some well-proven combinations and tips on how to get the best from your choice.

Over the past ten years Partiblend has become recognised as one of the best carpet attractors. As soon as this combination of fourteen mini particles hits the lake bed its unique visual cloud begins to dissipate into the surrounding water. The seepage of milky, spicey and oily flavours will continue for up to 24 hours, leaving a trail of food messages across the lake for the carp to follow and home in on. Why not fish a tiger nut over the top? Carp love them! The high levels of inherent sugars and milk within tiger nuts, combined with their crunchiness and irregular shape have made them one of the cult particles of the 90's, and rightly so. One extra tip. Why not try two or three handfuls of our recently introduced Chopped Tiger Nuts with your bed of Partiblend. We believe that Chopped Tiger Nuts are up to three times more attractive than their whole conterparts. This makes them an ideal companion for Hinders Mega Hemp which is, in Matt Hayes's opinion, "The best fish attractor in the world!" So why not try fishing over a bed of Chopped Tiger Nuts and Mega Hemp?

The easiest way to personalise any particle is either to sprout them or flavour/colour them. To flavour/colour take three kilos dry weight of your chosen particle, tip into a large bucket, cover with warm water, add two desertspoons full of sugar and one level teaspoon of colouring then add the recommended level of flavour normally suggested for one kilo of base mix. Leave to soak overnight, stirring occasionally. Cook in the water used for soaking. When cool the particles are ready for use, or they can be frozen into session-sized packs.

Certain particles lend themselves more easily to sprouting. The easiest to try is chick peas. Take a large tray lined with a sodden towel. Cover the towel evenly with chick peas and sprinkle a small amount of sugar over them. Cover the chick peas with a second wet towel and place in a warm dry place (an airing cupboard is ideal). It is important the towels remain saturated throughout. Check the chick peas every twelve hours until there is about a quater of an inch of sprout showing. The chick peas now need to be prepared as recommended in our full, easy to follow, safe preparation guide issued with each order of Hinders particles.

Although not generally perceived to be a particle, trout pellets have increasingly been used to great success. Hinders have been at the forefront of the trout pellet explosion, introducing an unrivalled range of over 11 different types ranging from 3mm to 14mm. The formulations of the Elips and the 14mm Mega Sinker contain Betaine and 90% digestible fishmeals making them irresistable and with a certain 'edge'. Following outstanding results during field testing we are making available the 4mm Mini Betaine pellet.

There is a misconception that because trout pellets contain oil they are dangerous to carp. If you fire in some trout pellets you will notice that an oil slick appears on the surface of the water creating instant attraction. Within minutes the oil will begin to wash out into the surrounding water. This reduces the percentage consumed by the carp but compels them to stay in the swim as the pellets continue to breakdown over the length of time dictated by your pellet size.

Here are some top tips for major results. Four to five hours before your session, submerge 4mm Mini Trout Pellets into your cooked hemp, or fill a PVA bag with 3mm Micro Sinkers and five or six Elips Pellets, together with your lead and Elips hookbait coated with clear nail varnish. The smell of the varnish will soon disappear and you can cast out knowing that you have a hookbait that will remain intact on the lake bed for many hours.

New for this year is the rapid breakdown Hemp Pellet. To retain the freshness 100% pure hempseed is crushed then immediately pelletised. Needing no further preparation they begin to fizz when immersed and break down totally within five minutes leaving a bed of finest crushed hemp. There is a distinct change in water colour around the broken down pellet and when the fish investigates the bed is disturbed creating a blizzard of crushed hemp. They can be catapulted further than ordinary hemp seeds, spodded or fished in PVA bags without the complication of the bag melting before you cast.

The concept of ball pellets has really taken off in the last few years. Our latest innovation is three different ball pellets incorporating Hinders ground trout pellets, tiger nuts or hemp seed. These address the problem of fishing crushed particles accurately and can be fired out further than conventional pellets. Also there is the advantage of not being able to over-feed the fish. Average breakdown time is about twenty five minutes and the energy fish expend in foraging is greater than the food content available, thus inducing them to search out more food and increasing the chances of a take.

Top Tip: cut a three inch square from a pair of fine nylon tights. Place a ball pellet in the centre and gather the corners together twisting tightly until the material is fully stretched over the pellet. Tie a slip knot with dental floss, secure with super glue and tie the ends to the ring on your hook giving you the same presentation as your free offerings. You can also present your hookbait on a three inch hooklink inside a PVA bag filled with ball pellets.

No article would be complete without mentioning groundbaits, an increasingly important component in the carp angler's bait armoury, especiallly with the advent of The Method fishing. Hinders 'A' Mix is a pure blend of assorted nuts and hemp crushed together to create a self-binding groundbait. The very high oil content of the ingredients gives it an allure and proves a constant fascination to the fish.

Another high-performance groundbait is Hinders Ultimate. This has achieved the two aims of formulating an all year round groundbait which can be used for The Method or as a straight bed attractor, without the drawbacks of over feeding the fish. The complex mix of ground trout pellets, assorted crushed seeds, fishmeals, pure extracts, appetite stimulators and flavour enhancers create a sweet, fruity overtone. Because Ultimate contains so many strong tasting ingredients, fish are enticed to move in from range, even in winter.

If you want the best of both worlds, mix the 'A' Mix 50/50 with the Ultimate. By rubbing the two groundbaits into each other you will transfer some of the massively high percentage of natural oils from the 'A' Mix to the Ultimate. The two bind together superbly and once on the lake bed, will immediately begin to react and fizz, breaking down to leave a picnic of irresistible goodies. Both these can be enhanced further with the addition of our purpose-designed 'A' Mix additives in fruit or spice.

Top tip: put equal amounts of evaporated milk and 'A' Mix additive together.

Shake well and dampen your groundbait with the mixture before use.

Finally for those of you who make your own bait we have two base mixes which have given our field testers their best season ever, Super Mystic Fish and Super Mystic Bird. The level of appetite stimulator and enhancer in any base mix is critical to the overall success of the end product. It controls the smoothness of taste, the palatability and it creates the desire for prolonged feeding spells. We have gone to great lengths to source and produce the right combination and levels of aminos/enhancers in our base mixes. These two recipes are the most popular with our field testers:

1) SUPER MYSTIC FISH.
6 large eggs
7ml Scopex
10ml Sense Appeal
20ml Hinders Super Salmon Oil
1ml Protaste Sweetener
Super Mystic Fish Base Mix

2) SUPER MYSTIC BIRD.
6 large eggs
5ml JB Buttringer
3ml JB Plum
15ml JB Amino Liver
1.5ml Protaste Sweetener
Super Mystic Bird Mix.

A full range of ingredients, fishmeals, birdfoods, milk proteins, pure extracts and the newly introduced, hemp oil, Betaine and Green Lipped Mussel is readily

available for the chefs among you to formulate your own dream bait. All the products mentioned in the article are on display at our Particle, Tackle and Bivvy Centre or are available nationwide though our dependable mail order service. For our latest catalogue telephone our brochure hotline on 01793-821377.

BILL COTTAM OF NUTRABAITS – INGREDIENTS FOR SUCCESS

To be perfectly honest, my views about bait don't differ in any way to those Ken has expressed in this book. Ken started his carp fishing way back in the 60's when I was still in nappies so he has been around the block once or twice and is certainly among the most experienced of all bait orientated carp men I know. Not only that, he started carping in Kent, of all places, the original melting pot for so many good bait ideas that have stood the test of time.

When you look at the current crop of angling writers there are really only a handful of people still writing authoritatively about bait and of them I'd guess that 90% of them have been around since the 70' and early 80's when the development of technology was running flat out in overdrive. When Tim Paisley, Nick Elliot and I first started talking bait, Ken was naturally one of the first anglers in the country to be asked to field test some of Tim's advanced ideas. His success and that enjoyed by a handful of other anglers in Kent and Yorkshire, was to pave the way for Nutrabaits which Tim and I started in early 1987. Now more than ten years on, I have to pinch myself from time to time to remind myself that this is not a dream.

Bait firms come and bait firms go and luckily Nutrabaits seems to get stronger and stronger. I believe this is mainly due to our research and development program which allows us to thoroughly field test new products in the hands of top class anglers such as Ken, Julian Cundiff, Brian Skoyles and Paul Selman, to name but four members of an outstanding team. We never put a product onto the market without giving it the most demanding work-over and only when we are satisfied that we have a product worthy of the Nutrabaits name will we go into full production with it.

In addition I get fantastic support from my good friend, business partner and long time (some would say, too long!) carp angler Richard Skidmore, as well as from our factory manager, Andy James, who has probably forgotten more about bait than most people learn in a lifetime. Nutrabaits employees Lee Walton and Pat Webb are constant sources of information and advice, and without the likes of Dave Moore, who developed Big Fish Mix for us, and a whole host of other unsung heros, Nutrabaits would not be where it is today.

As Ken has already mentioned elsewhere in the book, the entire philosophy of Nutrabaits revolves around the concept of providing a valid food source with highly attractive flavours and other feeding and appetite stimulants. It is all too easy just to throw any old junk in a mixing bowl and call it a bait, but that is most definitely not the way we look at it.

There is no getting away from the fact that carp eat bait. They do so because anglers have taught them that little round balls of strange smelling stuff is food. We have done this by developing flavours and attractors that trial and error has shown to be highly effective. For instance, you probably know that most fruit flavours attract carp, not because they smell of fruit, but because they smell of something that the carp either learns to associate with food, or by some quirk of nature, is already associated with it naturally.

We add flavours to provide a label to our food source so that, in time, carp recognise the smell and recall eating something that smelled the same, not long ago, which they enjoyed.

Any bait company will tell you, all the flavours and smells we use are origi-nally intended for the food industry which spends millions of pounds a year on artificial commercially produced flavour products. The industry uses these to sim-ulate tastes and smells that humans enjoy. For the most part that means that just about any flavour will be acceptable to the comparatively insensitive human senses. That is most definitely not the case with carp. Again the bait trade will tell you that some smells catch carp better than others and as Ken has pointed out in the book, some esters, amines and chemical bases can become recognised to such an extent that their very presence spells danger (see also Kevin's earlier section in this chapter). That is one reason why we tend to use more glycerol-based flavours in the Nutrabaits range, glycerol being far less widely used in the food trade due to its high cost. Because it is less widely available to carp anglers, there is less chance of a glycerol based flavour blowing.

Glycerol has the added advantage of being a much softer base which rounds of the flavour to give a very smooth finished product. Just open a bottle of Strawberry Nutrafruit and compare its smell to any other strawberry flavour on the market. I think you'll see what I mean. Then try the tongue test; dip the tip of your little finger into the lid of the bottle to take a minute quantity onto your finger, then touch the finger to the tip of your tongue. You will note that flavours based on say, propylene glycol, will produce a sharp burning sensation on the tongue, whereas the glycerol-based Nutrafruit will give far less burn than other strawberry flavours based on less sophisticated solvent bases.

It can take many years to develop a flavour to its full extent so that its poten-tial can be realised most effectively. For instance, we have recently accepted a more refined and sophisticated glycerol based version of Salmon Elite which we think is a big improvment on the previous version. This seems to be borne out by the results some of our field testers have enjoyed as the feedback from them has been very encouraging. What has been particularly noticeable about the new version is its superb qualities as a winter flavour/attractor; something the Mark One version was not. Recent experiments suggest that a blend of 4ml/lb of both Caviar and the new Salmon Elite will be an oustandingly good combination.

It is this policy of rigorous testing that gives us the confidence to offer prod-ucts that are known catchers. Take the Total Hemp range. Now everybody knows that hemp is attractive to carp, they also know what a wind-up it can be to prepare enough of the stuff to keep one hungry carp satisfied, let alone a dozen or more. So when we asked a processor if he could manufacture pure hemp as a compressed pellet we were delighted when he said yes. Testing took place throughout 1997 and now we are confident that we can launch the product onto the market in the certain knowledge that it will increase the attraction present in anybody's swim.

This gave us pause for thought. How effective would a hemp-based boiled bait be if fished over the top of a carpet of Total Hemp Pellets? Pretty good, we thought. But have you ever tried to bind, then roll a boilie mix that comprises 80% pure crushed hemp ingredients. Next to impossible, right?

It has taken our staff and the field testers many frustrating hours to find a suit-able combination of attractors, vitamins, minerals and binders to form the Total

Andy James, who manages the day-to-day running of the Nutrabaits warehouse.

Hemp Boilie Mix but the effort has been worth it. We have been using the hemp based products throughout the last twelve months or so, and I must say, even I am amazed at how effective they have been. OK, you don't need to be a genius to understand why: hemp is brilliant whatever form it comes in, but if you haven't witnessed for yourself the glorious sight of carp tearing up the bottom to get at the soft mush of hemp – the result of the dissolving Total Hemp Pellets – you just haven't lived!

Our research has also led us to introduce two other products of which one is our first specialist groundbait which Ken has briefly mentioned elsewhere. Originally we were looking at a tench/bream/general match groundbait for use on really busy stockie waters teeming with the small carp that match anglers prefer, but in the process we have come up with a groundbait that is particularly suited to the carp and specialist angler. The Specialist Carpet Feed is the result. Because of the feed's make up you will find that you need very little liquid in order to bind it into catapult sized balls. In fact, some of our testers have been using neat liquid foods such as Multimino-PPC as the liquid content which is an awesome combination. We also like to use the Specialist Carpet Feed for fishing The Method, using one of the specially designed feeders currently on offer from Richworth or Essential Products. Like any tactic, The Method works only as well as the attractors, in this case those incorporated into the groundbait. Because of its highly attractive contents and built-in oil and attractor package, our Specialist Carpet Feed is ideally suited to fishing The Method. However, don't limit yourself to just one method, or just one tactic. On the right waters a sloppy mixture of Carpet Feed and Total Hemp Pellets introduced to the margins will inevitably draw carp very close in where they can be intercepted right under the rod tips.

Another outstanding introduction into our range is the Ball Pellets. These have been doing the business since their introduction in 1997. We designed complimentary Ball Pellet Sprays to add even further to their attractiveness and it has been our experience, both on UK waters and abroad, that Ball Pellets work best when used in combination with a scattering of boiled baits. I know Ken swears by a ratio of two-thirds Ball Pellets: one-third boiled baits. We now believe that the days of Boilie Crumb and Boilie Soup may be numbered. You can do so much more with Ball Pellets, Hemp Pellets and Carpet Feed which are much more versatile

Our continuing commitment to make top class bait technology available to all has given me personally a great deal of satisfaction. Our own club formed especially for Nutrabaits users, Club Nutrabaits, has been an amazing success story and I only have to read the letters that flood in from both youngsters and established anglers alike to know that Nutrabaits is regarded as one of the the most helpful and approachable of companies. It is my hope that we shall continue to offer the same level of support and service in the years to come, and with the help of guys like Ken and the rest of our dedicated team we shall continue to bring you the very latest advances that will help you land the big carp of your dreams.

Good luck!